NOIR CITY

THIS ISSUE

NO. 38 | 2023

NOIR CITY

ISSUE 38

PUBLISHER Eddie Muller
EDITOR IN CHIEF Imogen Sara Smith
MANAGING EDITORS Danilo Castro,
Steve Kronenberg
ART DIRECTOR/DESIGNER Michael Kronenberg
PROMOTIONAL DIRECTOR Daryl Sparks
CONTRIBUTORS THIS ISSUE Sean Axmaker, Randy
Dotinga, Mary Mallory, Vance McLaughlin, Rich Taus,
Rachel Walther, Andy Wolverton, John Wranovics
COMMUNICATIONS DIRECTOR Anne Hockens
SOCIAL MEDIA COORDINATOR Danilo Castro
WEBSITE / E-SERVICES Ted Whipple

FILM NOIR FOUNDATION BOARD OF DIRECTORS
Eddie Muller, President; Board members:
Foster Hirsch, Brian Hollins, Andrea Kasin,
Anita Monga, Alan K. Rode

ADVISORY COUNCIL Dana Delany, Gwen Deglise,
James Ellroy, Bruce Goldstein, Vince Keenan, John Kirk,
Dennis Lehane, Leonard Maltin, Rose McGowan, Jon
Mysel, Fernando Martín Peña, Michael Schlesinger,
Imogen Sara Smith, Todd Wiener

FILM NOIR FOUNDATION

The Film Noir Foundation is a non-profit public benefit corporation created by Eddie Muller in 2005 as an educational resource regarding the cultural, historical, and artistic significance of film noir as an international cinematic movement. It is the foundation's mission to find and preserve films in danger of being lost or irreparably damaged, and to ensure that high-quality prints of these classic films remain in circulation for theatrical exhibition to future generations. Once these films are unearthed, restored, and returned to circulation, the chances increase that the films will be made available on Blu-ray and/or via online streaming for future generations of film lovers to appreciate.

To date, the Film Noir Foundation has fully funded the restorations of *The Prowler* (1951), *Cry Danger* (1951), *Try and Get Me!* (1951), *Too Late for Tears* (1949), *Woman on the Run* (1950), *The Guilty* (1947), *Los tallos amargos* (1956, Argentina), *The Man Who Cheated Himself* (1950), *Trapped* (1949), *La bestia debe morir* (1952, Argentina), and *El vampiro negro* (1953, Argentina), and *The Argyle Secrets* (1948). The Foundation has initiated and partially underwritten the restoration of *Repeat Performance* (1947) and *High Tide* (1947), and financed 35mm preservations of *Nobody Lives Forever* (1946), *Three Strangers* (1946), *High Wall* (1947), *The Hunted* (1948), *The Window* (1949), *Southside 1-1000* (1950), *Roadblock* (1951), *Down Three Dark Streets* (1954), *Loophole* (1954), *The Underworld Story* (1950), and *Cry Tough* (1959), plus the Argentine films *Apenas un delincuente* (1949), *No abras nunca esa puerta* (1952), and *Si muero antes de despertar* (1952). Currently, in partnership with UCLA Film & Television Archive, the FNF is proceeding with the digital restoration of another Argentine film after receiving the long-awaited film elements in late March. This latest restoration will premiere in 2024 on the NOIR CITY film festival circuit.

NOIR CITY, the FNF's Bay Area flagship festival, began in January 2003. It has grown into the largest film noir–specific yearly event in the United States, the centerpiece of the Film Noir Foundation's public awareness campaign. Viewers have been drawn to this NOIR CITY every year (except 2021) from all over the world, eager to immerse themselves in a extravaganza of rare films, special guests, music, literary tie-ins—a communal celebration of all things noir.

Please consider supporting our mission with a donation to the Film Noir Foundation.

GREYSCALE

BIN TRAVELER FORM

Cut By _Henay_ # _25_ Qty _23_ Date _10·07_

Scanned By _____ Qty _____ Date _____

Scanned Batch IDs

Notes / Exception

TCM
NOIR ALLEY

HOSTED BY NOIR EXPERT
EDDIE MULLER

SATURDAYS AT MIDNIGHT ET WITH AN ENCORE ON **SUNDAYS** AT 10AM ET

VISIT TCM.COM/NOIRALLEY

See *I Wouldn't Be in Your Shoes* (1948)
and other Film Noir Classics each week on TCM

THE
CRITERION
CHANNEL

A Noir Lover's Dream

Madeleine, directed by David Lean

America's Gross Domestic Product is Crime

If you don't believe me, just peruse a daily paper—if you can still find one. Newspapers have long been divided into five sections: "News" could now be more precisely called "Crime and Corruption," since that's what lurks behind every national story involving politics and economics. The "Metro" section features local news—typically a litany of murder and manslaughter and the occasional tragic accident. "Sports"—once a respite—can barely camouflage the rampant greed of billionaire owners and violent abuses of star athletes. The "Business" section—where the most egregious crimes are on display—is beyond the comprehension of John Q. Public. The ever-shrinking "Arts & Entertainment" section once offered sanctuary, but these days most of the stories we're being told—if they aren't superhero fantasies—are "based on a true story." And 99 percent of those involve crime, be it institutional or intimate.

I've long maintained that the original noir era, an explosion of artist-inspired creativity in the wake of the Great Depression and World War II, represented the on-screen expression of America's loss of innocence. In the first paragraph of the first book I ever wrote on the subject, I called many of these films "warning flares launched by artists working the night shift at the Dream Factory." The irony is that they were made during a time when the Motion Picture Production Code policed what was considered appropriate viewing. Movies based on true crimes were few and far between—not because there weren't heinous crimes committed daily in this country, but because in the studio era there was a much closer connection between the federal government, Wall Street, and Hollywood. Control was exerted over the stories presented to the public, and those stories reflected who we *wanted* to be, more than who we actually were.

Back then, artists didn't advertise that a story was based on fact. The notorious 1928 case of adulterous murderer Ruth Snyder may have inspired James M. Cain to write *The Postman Always Rings Twice* (published in 1934, not made into a Hollywood film until 1946), but neither its publisher, Alfred A. Knopf, nor MGM promoted the book or film as "based on a true story." The same held true for many classic works of noir, literary and cinematic. Writers would be intrigued by an actual crime and adapt it into a fictionalized narrative. Sensitive readers and viewers could always assure themselves these tales were merely dark fantasies. They didn't have anything to do with our family, friends, and colleagues. Right?

Things began to change during the noir era, and that's what we explore in this issue of NOIR CITY. I offer a survey of "true crime" movies from the classic era. Editor Imogen Sara Smith brings her typically keen insight to a consideration of how the visual representation of crime evolved over the years. Danilo Castro looks at an array of cold cases that have gotten big-screen treatments. Did you know *The Night of the Hunter* (1955), *Targets* (1968), and *Dog Day Afternoon* (1975) are all based on true crimes? We provide the factual backstories of these landmark movies.

I wish we could say that America heeded those mid-century "warning flares." The fact that there's no escape from crime, in our lives or in our entertainment, would seem to indicate that Americans aren't good learners. Or maybe we're just criminals at heart.

Darkly yours,

—*Eddie Muller*

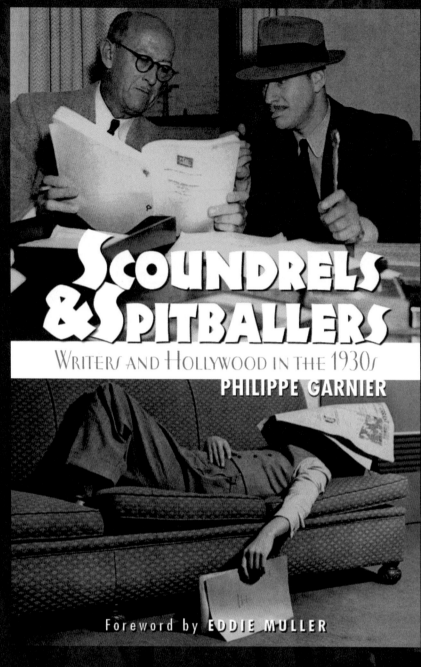

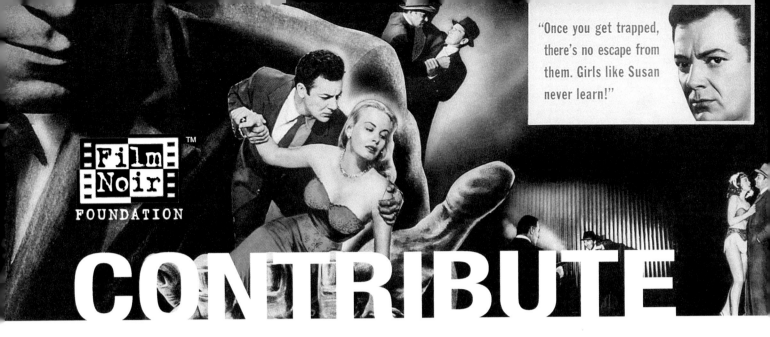

"Once you get trapped, there's no escape from them. Girls like Susan never learn!"

CONTRIBUTE

Film noir's rain-slicked streets, shadowy alleys, and sex bombs in silk peignoirs deserve a permanent place on the BIG screen. But hey, "it's a bitter little world," and we can't do it alone. We need your donations to help us locate, restore, and exhibit these films before they're lost forever. Do it for the love of noir—but enjoy the thank-you gifts, too!

HOW TO CONTRIBUTE TO THE FILM NOIR FOUNDATION
Please see contribution levels listed on the right and the associated gifts for each.

NOTE: If no gifts are desired, you may indicate such and you will receive a 100% tax deduction.

Option 1 - Make your donation ONLINE from the FNF's contribute page via PayPal (yes, you can use your credit card) at https://www.filmnoirfoundation.org/contribute.html

Option 2 - Make your donation via CHECK and mail to:

Film Noir Foundation
1411 Paru Street
Alameda, CA 94501

Important: IN ORDER TO RECEIVE THE NOIR CITY E-MAG, DONORS MUST SIGN UP ON THE FNF MAILING LIST at **https://www.filmnoirfoundation.org/signup.html**

Note: Does your PayPal address differ from your mailing list email address? If your PayPal email address differs from the email address provided for our mailing list, be sure to let us know, so you will be included in the NOIR CITY e-mag broadcasts.

PLEASE ALLOW AT LEAST FOUR WEEKS FOR DELIVERY OF DONOR THANK YOU GIFTS. Be sure to provide your mailing address to receive merchandise. Apologies, but we cannot ship donor thank-you packages outside the United States

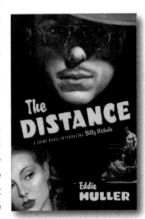

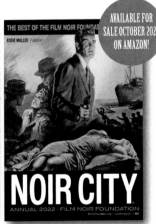

AVAILABLE FOR SALE OCTOBER 2023 ON AMAZON!

Get the NOIR CITY® e-magazine

A donation of $20 or more entitles you to receive a 1-year subscription to the *NOIR CITY* e-magazine, published every four months in electronic format, and sent as a downloadable link in an email to donors who have signed up on the mailing list. IMPORTANT: You must sign up for the *NOIR CITY* e-magazine at filmnoirfoundation.org/signup.html in order to receive the electronic publication.

SHAMUS
$20 to $49
Receive the *NOIR CITY* Magazine - digital version (e-mail address required).

MUSCLE
$50 - $99
Receive the *NOIR CITY* Magazine - digital version - and the most recent NOIR CITY festival poster.

HENCHMAN
$100 - $249
All of the above, plus the 2023 NOIR CITY 20 Souvenir Program and a copy of the NOIR CITY Annual 15 (published 2023).

TORPEDO
$250 - $499
Receive all of the above plus a signed first edition of Eddie Muller's novel, *The Distance*.

KINGPIN
$500+
The whole shebang plus a NOIR CITY Passport (all-access pass) to NOIR CITY 21 at Oakland's Grand Lake Theatre, January 19 - 28, 2024.

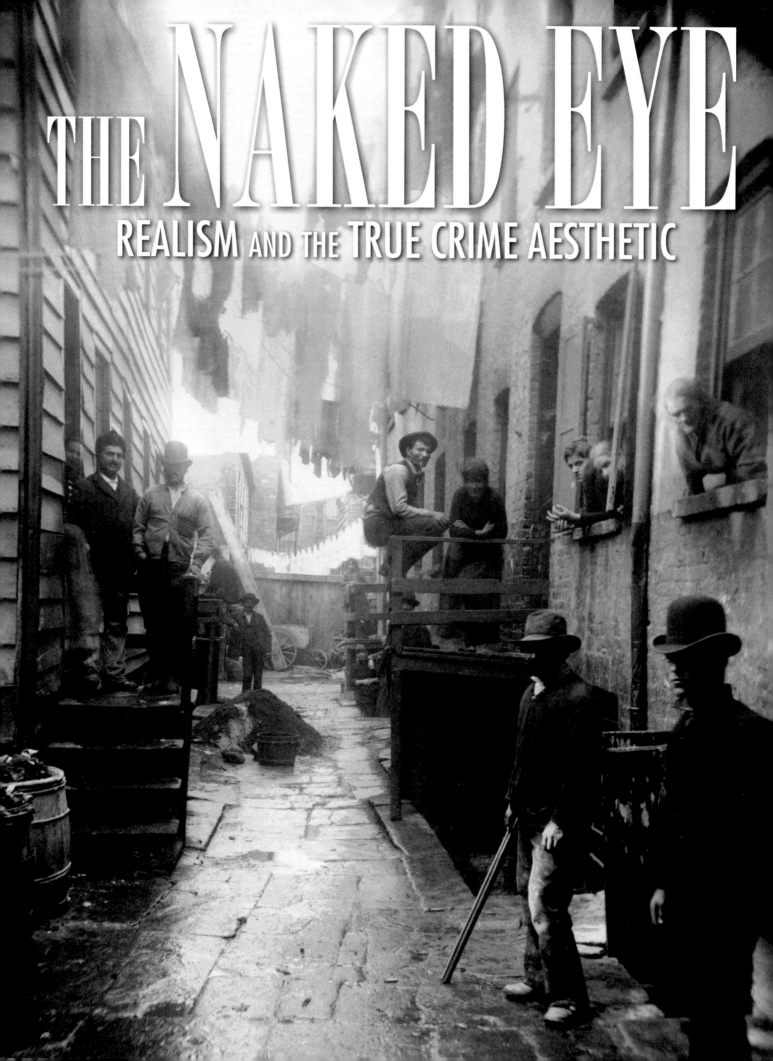

THE NAKED EYE

REALISM AND THE TRUE CRIME AESTHETIC

By Imogen Sara Smith

S ince the invention of cinema, movies have fed two contradictory yet entangled desires: for fact and fantasy, truth and magic, realism and escape. Cinema began with the *actualités* of the Lumière brothers, which documented real people, real streets, real trains; and the *féeries* of Georges Méliès, which harnessed the camera's ability to visualize the impossible and the fantastic. These approaches seem like stark opposites, but every film has aspects of both. Even the most scrupulous cinéma verité transforms its subject with framing and editing; even the most stylized Hollywood musical is a record of something that happened in front of a camera.

Film noir is associated with expressionistic stylization and the artifice of Hollywood studio filmmaking, but also with "gritty realism." After World War II, crime dramas were at the forefront of a movement to bring documentary elements into the dream factory—location shooting, natural lighting, and narratives based on fact. But the relationship between a realist aesthetic and true crime stories goes back much further, encompassing a host of visual influences and techniques in the quest for veracity. Here are three examples of the dissenting strain that has always pushed against the movies' preference for beautiful make-believe.

Raoul Walsh's *Regeneration* captured the menace of New York's Lower East Side slums with gritty flair, recalling Jacob Riis's iconic 1888 photograph "Bandits' Roost, 59 ½ Mulberry Street" (left), an image that Martin Scorsese later reproduced in *Gangs of New York* (2002).

How the Other Half Lives: *Regeneration* (1915)

Considered the first full-length gangster movie, *Regeneration* was based on *My Mamie Rose* (1903), the colorful autobiography of Owen Frawley Kildare, a self-described "beer slinger and pugilist in a tough Bowery dive." Kildare (the name may have been a pseudonym) recounted growing up as an abused orphan on the Lower East Side and running with a street gang until his life was transformed by a woman who worked at a local settlement house, who taught him to read and encouraged his early efforts at writing. The popular book was a tribute to this savior, who tragically died of pneumonia a week before they were to be married. A stage adaptation in 1908 gave the story a punchier ending where the saintly woman is killed by a gangster's bullet, and Owen bears responsibility for ensnaring her in his old life. Kildare's dismay at this twisting of the facts seems to have contributed to a mental breakdown, and by the time Raoul Walsh (with cowriter Carl Harbaugh) turned the play into a movie, retaining this violent climax, the author had died in a state hospital.

Regeneration, Walsh's directorial debut after working as an actor and assistant to D. W. Griffith, was a hit with both critics and audiences, solidly establishing his career. He shot the film in New York, recruiting real street characters—hoodlums, prostitutes, Bowery bums—as extras. (According to legend, Griffith had used real gangsters in his 1912 short film *The Musketeers of Pig Alley*.) Walsh had grown up in Manhattan, but in a privileged setting closer to that of the uptown swells in the film who come down to the Bowery

Raoul Walsh gave up acting after he lost his right eye in 1928, thanks to a jackrabbit that hit the windshield of his car while he was driving in Arizona.

on a slumming trip. He went hog-wild playing up the squalor of the slums, packing the film with grotesquely disfigured faces and disabled or obese bodies. In the tenements, young Owen grows up surrounded by cracked and peeling walls, shredded curtains, broken chairs, ragged drunks swilling beer from tin pails, and dirty toddlers playing in greasy, littered stairwells.

The look of *Regeneration* recalls both the photographs of social reformer Jacob Riis, whose *How the Other Half Lives* (1890) shocked viewers by exposing the abject poverty in New York's slums, and the paintings of the Ashcan School. Around the turn of the twentieth century, artists like George Bellows and George Luks painted street scenes, tenements, boxing clubs, saloons, docks, and construction sites, celebrating the vigor and vitality of working-class urban life, a style Walsh echoed with red-blooded brio. Working with French cinematographer Georges Benoît, he captured marvelous scenes of swarming streets, kids playing on fire escapes, docks jostling with cranes and tugboats. An excursion-boat disaster based on the 1904 sinking of the General Slocum is staged with alarming verisimilitude, with extras leaping off the ship to escape raging flames—though the sequence is given an ahistorical happy ending ("All the kiddies were saved").

Against this backdrop of raw realism, the central story of moral reformation feels even more creakily Victorian, especially the flawless nobility and purity of Marie (i.e., "Mamie Rose"), played by the angelically beautiful Anna Q. Nilsson. The stage actor Rockliffe Fellowes is charismatic as Owen, even if he seems a little too affable and clean-cut to be leading a gang of thugs. The villain, Skinny (William Sheer), is a far more persuasive lowlife, with his gaunt face, ratlike teeth, and eye patch (eerily prefiguring the one Walsh would

WILLIAM SHEER

William Sheer in "Regeneration."

Appearing in

William Fox Productions

English-born actor William Sheer appeared in a handful of films in the 1910s but is remembered almost exclusively for *Regeneration* (also known as *The Regeneration*).

According to his brother, Robert E. Burns suffered from what we would now term PTSD after his service in World War I, leading him to become a drifter.

wear after losing an eye in 1928). The plot change that so upset Kildare greatly strengthens the story: Owen's dilemma when Skinny pleads for protection after knifing a cop pits old debts and deep-rooted loyalties against his desire to keep Marie's respect. His choice has dire consequences, leading to a fatal showdown between the two men when Skinny assaults Marie.

Walsh's mastery of action is displayed in a magnificent long shot capturing Skinny's attempt to escape via one of the dozens of clotheslines stretched between two cliff-like tenements. But nothing prepares you for the shock close-up after he falls: his face a gruesome death mask with blood running from the mouth, one eye wide open and the other a hollow socket. Movies would wrestle for decades with how graphic they should be, and while they have ultimately come down on the side of explicitness, the question remains: how much realism do audiences want, and how much truth can they handle?

No Escape: I Am a Fugitive from a Chain Gang (1932) and 1930s Social Realism

Prohibition, which took effect in 1920, had many unintended consequences: it spawned an enormous rise in organized crime and gangland violence, and the nation's fascination with the underworld in turn boosted the genre of true crime. In 1924, editor Bernarr Mac-fadden founded the pioneering *True Detective Mysteries*, initially publishing a mix of fiction and nonfiction stories. Around 1930, he phased out the fiction to focus solely on true crime. Accounts of Prohibition-era violence, and the pulp stories and hard-boiled novels

inspired by them—like the two classic books James M. Cain spun out of Ruth Snyder's 1927 plot to murder her husband—would provide fodder for many postwar noir films.

In 1931, *True Detective Mysteries* serialized a sensational first-person story by Robert Elliott Burns, which was published in book form in 1932 as *I Am a Fugitive from a Chain Gang!* and turned into a film the same year at Warner Bros., directed by Mervyn LeRoy. Burns, who was sentenced to ten years' hard labor for a petty stickup that he insisted he had been tricked into by an acquaintance, exposed the hellish conditions in southern prison camps, from which he had twice escaped. LeRoy's film, lensed by Sol Polito and anchored by Paul Muni's searing performance, has a rough, drab, documentary look, and wisely makes no attempt to inject any lightness or humor into the story. Although the film spans the end of World War I to the present, the whole affair is suffused with a Depression-era mood of desperation and hopelessness. Muni's character, renamed James Allen, seems trapped from the get-go, when he flees a soul-crushing factory job to become a drifter. The single mistake that dooms him is trying to run when the cops burst in during the stickup; because of it, he must keep running forever.

Committed to authenticity, Muni met with Burns, who served as a consultant on the film, and studied the way he walked and talked, aiming to capture the "smell of fear" that clung to him. (Burns was still wanted in Georgia, but the film's success emboldened him to make public appearances denouncing the chain-gang system.) Muni also did intensive research into the southern penal system, meeting with guards who had worked at camps like the ones depicted. He gives his most naturalistic performance, matching the film's verité style, which relies on archival stock footage to give the feeling of a newsreel. As Allen wanders the country, he encounters nothing but trains, construction sites, flophouses, lunch wagons, and pawn shops overflowing with medals hocked by veterans.

Once he gets to the prison camp, the movie takes its time letting us absorb the full horror. We observe how the convicts' shackles are hammered on and checked each day, and the awkward way the chains force them to hobble. We see how the work gangs are loaded onto trucks in the predawn darkness; and how long "bull chains" are run through rings on the men's shackles, pulled through with a chilling sound like a metallic death rattle. We see the convicts spread

> " Nothing prepares you for the shock close-up after he falls: his face a gruesome death mask with blood running from the mouth, one eye wide open and the other a hollow socket.

In 1932, Paul Muni was Oscar-nominated for his performance as James Allen, and the same year played the brutal gangster Tony Camonte in Howard Hawks's *Scarface*.

Chicago-born Muni got his start in Yiddish Theatre as Muni Weisenfreund. An uncredited Everett Brown played Sebastian, the Black inmate who helps Allen escape.

out across the glaring sweep of a quarry, breaking rocks in the heat and dust. In a period when most Hollywood films were still studio-bound, these scenes display the kind of unvarnished candor seen in photographs of Dustbowl migrants taken for the Farm Security Administration by artists such as Dorothea Lange and Margaret Bourke-White. During Allen's first escape, suspense is heightened by the lack of music, natural setting, and stripped-down urgency: there is only the sound of dogs baying and blurry traveling shots as he pelts through dusty, sun-splashed underbrush.

His liberty is short-lived, since he is blackmailed into marriage by a gold-digging woman who threatens to turn him in if he leaves her. Having become a successful engineer, he tells another woman that he wants to build roads and bridges so that people can get away. (In reality, after his first escape Burns became a newspaper editor.) When Allen is tricked into returning voluntarily to captivity—assured he will get a pardon if he serves sixty days, only to find that Georgia intends to make him serve out his full ten years of hard labor as revenge for his exposure of the system—he manages to escape again. His disillusionment is symbolized by his blowing up a bridge during his getaway, destroying what he had hoped to build.

I Am a Fugitive from a Chain Gang was not only a critical success, praised for its "stark realism" and "unflinching realism," and

nominated for a bouquet of awards; it was also a big moneymaker for Warner Bros., proving wrong Roy Del Ruth, who had turned down an offer to direct the film on the grounds that it was the wrong time to make such a depressing movie, that audiences craved escape. The only people who did not like the film were prison authorities in Georgia, who protested that they had been unfairly maligned. Yet the movie does not even touch on the most shameful aspect of the "convict leasing" system: the fact that it was a source of revenue for the state, a legal form of slavery. As Allen cries out after being returned to the chain gang, "Their crimes are worse than anyone here."

Made at a time when the case was still unresolved, *I Am a Fugitive from a Chain Gang* is a rare example of a movie based on a true story whose ending is more downbeat than what really happened. Burns was arrested again in 1932, but the governor of New Jersey (Burns's home state, where he had returned) refused to extradite him; thanks to the book and the movie, public opinion was solidly on his side. The fugitive married again and started a family, finally obtaining a commutation of his sentence to time served in 1943, with the help of the newly elected Georgia governor Ellis Arnall. He lived out the rest of his life a free man.

The film forgoes any optimism, distilling all the pessimism and disillusionment of 1932—the worst year of the Depression—into one of the most powerful endings in cinema. After a montage of newspaper headlines speculating on the whereabouts of the fugitive, Allen materializes out of the night to speak with Helen (Helen Vinson), the woman he loves. In an anguished, ripped-from-the-guts speech, he tells her that even though he escaped, "They're still after me. They'll always be after me. I hide in rooms all day and travel by night. No friends, no rest, no peace. Keep moving, that's all that's left for me." She begs him to stay, but he retreats into the shadows, dissolving into the darkness as he slips away. "How do you live?" she asks, and his answer—"I steal!"—comes from a black void.

It is not always factual accuracy or documentary plainness that add up to truth: it takes art to make a moment so piercingly true to a whole nation's sense of loss, shame, and fear.

Just the Facts: *Call Northside 777* (1948) and Postwar Semidocumentaries

I Am a Fugitive from a Chain Gang could never have been made after 1934, when the Motion Picture Production Code began to be strictly enforced. While the Code only dealt with the content of movies, Hollywood films began to look different too: more polished, more classical, with all the rough edges sanded off. By the mid-1940s, after a decade of glossy and airless studio perfection, seeing real, ordinary places on screen was cause for excitement. One of the most enthusiastic champions of the postwar movement to bring documentary elements into movies was writer James Agee, who lavishly praised

Elia Kazan's *Boomerang!* (1947), one of the earliest examples of the trend. That same year, he wrote, "One of the best things that is happening in Hollywood is the tendency to move out of the place—to base fictional pictures on fact, and, more importantly, to shoot them not in painted studio sets but in actual places."

The public's appetite for realism had been whetted by the great combat documentaries made during World War II, while many film-

> **" By the mid-1940s, after a decade of glossy and airless studio perfection, seeing real, ordinary places on movie screens was cause for excitement.**

Betty Garde plays Wanda Skutnik, based on real-life witness Vera Walush, who wrongly identified the two men who shot a police officer in her Chicago speakeasy.

Call Northside 777 was James Stewart's first venture into film noir, while Richard Conte was a mainstay of crime dramas throughout the 1940s and '50s.

makers were inspired by the radical, emotionally shattering works of Italian neorealism (such as Vittorio De Sica's *Shoeshine* [1946] and *Bicycle Thieves* [1948]), which used nonprofessional actors and location shooting to tell stories stripped of any comforting illusions. Framing crime dramas with stentorian narrators boasting of films' adherence to facts, or prologues featuring sclerotic civil servants speechifying in their offices was also a way to appease the Production Code's requirement that movies uphold law, order, and virtue. It evidently didn't occur to the censors that audiences merely sat through these sermons in order to get to the good parts—gangsters, violence, seedy settings, and inky shadows.

The "semi-documentary" style ("pseudo-documentary" might be more accurate) took firm root at 20th Century Fox, thanks largely to producer Louis de Rochemont, the creator of the *March of Time* newsreel series. De Rochemont produced *Boomerang!*, and the studio followed up the next year with Henry Hathaway's *Call Northside 777*; both films were based on real cases of men wrongfully accused of crimes, and were shot on location, sometimes in the actual spots where the events had taken place. (See Eddie Muller's survey on page 26 for a discussion of Kazan's film; and see the review of *Nothing to Fear* on page 74 for hair-raising statistics on the frequency of wrongful convictions due to police corruption and misconduct in the mid-twentieth century.) Focusing on innocent men whose names are eventually cleared was a way to make crime movies under the Production Code that could have happy endings; but exposing the failures and callousness of the justice system directly challenged the Code's emphasis on showing respect for authorities and institutions. Insisting on these stories' factual basis only made the challenge bolder.

Call Northside 777 changed names but hewed fairly close to the facts in its account of a case that started in 1932 with the fatal shooting of a Chicago policeman in a speakeasy, part of the cresting wave of violent crime that finally led to the repeal of Prohibition one year later. Two men, Joseph Majczek and Theodore Marcinkiewicz, were convicted of the killing and had served eleven years in jail when, in 1944, two *Chicago Times* reporters spotted an ad placed by Majc-

zek's mother, Tillie, offering $5,000 for information on the killing. Smelling human interest in the story of a devoted mother who had saved the money by working as a scrubwoman, they delved into the case, their investigation ultimately leading to the men's release—though not to the identity of the real killer, who was never found. In the film, the reporter played by James Stewart starts out cynically dismissive, only gradually convinced that a gross injustice has been done as he discovers the men were railroaded on the dubious testimony of a single witness, the bitter and defiantly spiteful Wanda Skutnik (Betty Garde).

Joseph MacDonald's crisp cinematography makes excellent use of Chicago locations far afield from icons like the Wrigley Building. Stewart's legwork takes him through the city's Polish neighborhoods, with their shabby wood-frame houses and ornate Catholic churches, and on a crawl through the dive bars behind the stockyards, where you can smell the stale beer and sweat. He also experiences the oppressive sterility and surveillance of the panopticon in Joliet's Stateville Prison. The film has a newspaper's blend of diligent fact-gathering punched up with local color, boldface urgency, and op-ed pleading. Its documentary aesthetic is wedded to an enthusiastic faith in the promise of technology to uncover truth, which feels sadly antiquated today. The crucial piece of evidence that turns the tide comes from a journalistic photograph that is enlarged until the date on a newspaper can be read. (This twist was invented for the movie.) In another scene, Leonarde Keeler, the inventor of the polygraph, appears as himself, administering a lie-detector test to Frank Wiecek (Richard Conte, playing the character based on Majczek). The reliability of polygraph tests has since been called into question, but Conte gives the scene an intense, visceral charge as Wiecek tries to control his own breathing and pulse in order to prove his honesty.

You can't always judge whether movies are telling the truth from the way they look. Some films that veer far afield from realism have roots in factual cases, like the southern gothic fairy tale *The Night of the Hunter* (1955) (see page 38 for the story of the serial killer who inspired Mitchum's character, Harry Powell). Plenty of noir films used location shooting and documentary techniques to tell entirely fictional stories, like Jules Dassin's *The Naked City* (1948). Producer Mark Hellinger purchased the rights to the freelance press photographer Arthur Fellig's 1945 photobook just so that he could use the title, but Dassin recreated certain trademark images by the era's greatest snatcher of crime-scene pictures and poet laureate of urban gawking, who styled himself Weegee the Famous.

Today, when photos and videos can be made to lie, and movies increasingly rely on images animated by a computer rather than recorded by a camera, the distinction between fact and fantasy, reality and make-believe, keeps getting murkier. Many people seem not to care. That's the true crime. ∎

Call Northside 777 was the first Hollywood studio film to be shot on location in Chicago, including a memorable tour of the city's dive bars.

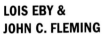

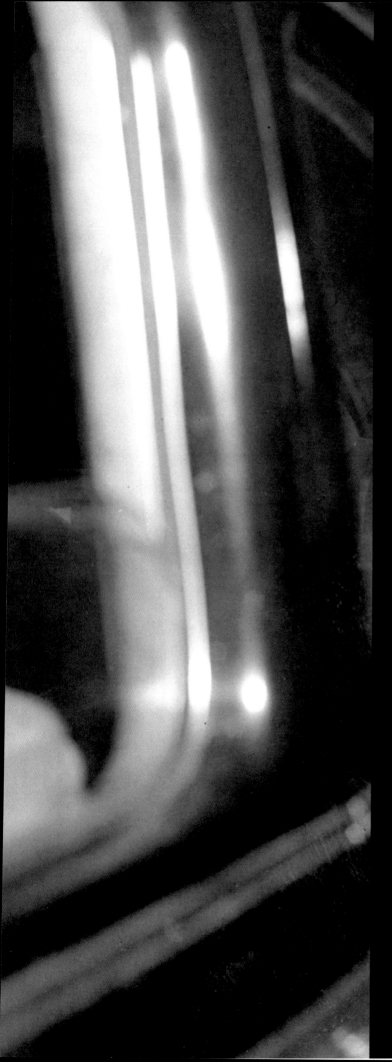

BURY THE PAST

Land Swindles. Chicago Mobsters. A Prison Break. A Suppressed Movie. And America's Cosmetics Kingpin? Take a wild ride through the tumultuous story of *Roger Touhy, Gangster*.

By John Wranovics

Maksymilian Faktorowicz, born in Poland in the 1870s, found initial success in Moscow, as a wigmaker. Later, after he'd moved to Los Angeles and changed his name to Max Factor, he claimed to have been the cosmetician for the czar of Russia's extended family, as well as the Imperial Russian Grand Opera. Attracted to the nascent Hollywood film industry, Max Factor established himself as a preeminent maker of theatrical cosmetics and wigs. He developed a new ultra-thin facial cream—ideal for film performers—which quickly replaced the thick, pasty make-up commonly used (and notorious for cracking). As color film emerged in the late 1920s, the new emulsion often cast a reddish tint on actors' made-up faces. Factor solved this by developing a new product called Pan-Cake. By the time he died in 1938, a demise hastened by a car accident two years earlier, Max Factor was known across America as the King of Cosmetics.

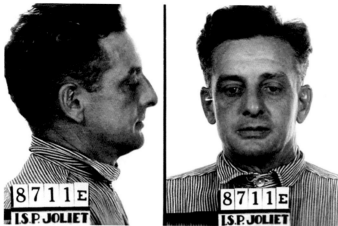

Roger Touhy, Chicago beer baron and Al Capone rival, spent twenty-five years in prison for the alleged kidnapping of John Factor.

Impressive. But it's Max Factor's younger half-brother, Iakov Faktorowicz, who holds more interest for this publication. His birthplace is uncertain—either England or Poland, probably sometime in late 1892. At the age of fourteen, Iakov would change his name to John Factor, after emigrating with his family to the United States and settling in St. Louis.

A born entrepreneur, John Factor started his career benignly, working as a newsboy, bootblack, and livery stable water boy. But his fortunes changed in 1916, when he moved to Chicago and opened a three-chair barber shop in Halsted Street on Chicago's West Side, charging only five cents for a haircut and a dime for a shave. By the late 1920s, he was simply known as "Jake the Barber." He used the shop's profits to promote oil land deals in the Southwest. A 1928 news item referred to him as "the notorious share pusher and arch swindler." Fellow crooks called him the "Master Crook of the Decade." John Factor soon moved into Florida real estate, selling $5 million worth of "ocean land." Indictments followed, as $1 million worth of that land was underwater.

To flee the heat, Jake the Barber secured the aid of New York racketeer Jack "Legs" Diamond, who grubstaked his escape to Europe. Apparently, the gangster and the "smooth-talking ex-barber" had an agreement under which Diamond financed Factor's swindles in exchange for a split of the profits. By some estimates

"In 1931, the Associated Press reported that Legs Diamond had put a price on Factor's head.

Factor pilfered anywhere from $5–12 million. But his big mistake was snubbing Diamond.

In 1931, the Associated Press reported that Diamond had put a price on Factor's head, and that the Barber "might be slain before he could be arrested for extradition to England, where he is accused of defrauding investors of several millions of dollars." Making Diamond even angrier was that during his trip to Europe to search for the elusive Factor, he was shot five times. Newspapers reported that "greedy gangsters . . . having heard that Factor had made $12,000,000, were seeking to kidnap him for ransom." News items declared that "gangs in New York, St. Louis, and Chicago had been hunting Factor for weeks to kidnap him, knowing he made millions in Europe and could pay huge ransoms—yet could not appeal to police for protection because the police wanted him also."

Factor eventually snuck back into Chicago and solicited protection from Al Capone. Meanwhile, he was tried in absentia in England and sentenced to twenty-four years in prison. Jake the Barber would fight his extradition all the way up until 1962, when President John F. Kennedy issued him a full pardon. It was later revealed that Factor was the single largest contributor to Kennedy's election campaign.

FLASHBACK: On April 18, 1933, Jake the Barber's son, Jerome, was kidnapped—the same day the US Supreme Court was hearing arguments about the Barber's extradition. Some believe the kidnapping had been faked in an attempt to stall the court's decision. If so, the ploy worked—the Supreme Court held the case over for reargument at a later date.

From the swamps of Florida to the casinos of London, Monte Carlo, and Las Vegas, Jake the Barber swindled his way to a fortune.

Perhaps inspired by the results of young Jerome's "kidnapping," Factor himself was reputedly kidnapped on June 30, 1933—at least, he disappeared for several weeks. Blame for the alleged crime was placed on a Cicero-based beer baron and Capone rival named Roger "the Terrible" Touhy, described in a 1933 newspaper exposé as "public enemy, alcohol czar, and roadhouse overlord."

On December 4, 1933, the Supreme Court ordered that John Factor be remanded to British authorities to face charges for fraudulent land swindles. He was taken into custody on April 17, 1934. But US Secretary of State Cordell Hull, encouraged by the Chicago police, arranged for Factor's release—so he could testify as a witness against Roger Touhy. A month prior, Touhy and some cronies had beaten the rap for the kidnapping of William A. Hamm, Jr., millionaire President of the Hamm Brewing Company. But on February 23, 1934, Touhy, Basil "The Owl" Banghart, and two others were convicted for Jake's alleged kidnapping. Touhy and Banghart were sentencedd to ninety-nine years at Stateville Prison in Joliet. For the rest of his life, Touhy argued that the kidnapping was a frame job orchestrated by his rival, Capone.

On October 9, 1942, the country was galvanized by news reports of Roger Touhy's escape from Stateville. Along with Banghart and five oth-

ers, Touhy had busted out with a few smuggled guns and a tall ladder. Within a week, according to the FBI, "[J. Edgar Hoover] directed a continent-wide man hunt that had no equal since the days of Dillinger." Touhy and his fellow escapees, however, were *state* prisoners—their escape violated no *federal* law. But the FBI was able to

After the FBI's Melvin Purvis failed to pin the Hamm kidnapping on Touhy (far right) and cronies, Touhy was the perfect fallguy for the John Factor snatch.

After three months on the lam, the FBI caught up with Touhy, killing two of his fellow prison escapees in the raid.

circumvent the jurisdictional issue since the fugitives failed to present themselves for registration under the Selective Service law, and draft dodging was a federal offense. The gang was soon captured by G-men in Chicago, with two of the escapees dying in the shootout. Banghart, confronted by Hoover, told the FBI director: "You're much fatter than you are on the radio." Touhy was returned to Stateville with 100 more years tacked on to his original 99 year sentence.

The Movie Version

By late 1942, mob-friendly producer Bryan Foy, now at 20th Century Fox after years heading the B unit at Warner Brothers, was developing *Prison Break*, the latest in a series of prison pictures made in collaboration with writer Crane Wilbur. Foy, a close friend of Capone operatives Johnny Roselli and Allen Smiley, immediately recognized the "ripped from the headlines" angle that Roger Touhy's bust-out presented, and the pair reshaped the project as *The Life of Touhy*. Lloyd Nolan, Victor McLaglen, Preston Foster, and Anthony Quinn were announced as stars—until a March 17, 1943, *Hollywood Reporter* item announced that Nolan, cast as Roger Touhy, was withdrawing to take "a stand against portraying any more screen gunmen." That May, studio PR noted that Quinn would play the informer Smoke Reardon, a role that ended up going to Henry Morgan. Quinn was cast instead as George Car-

roll, Touhy's Stateville cellmate. The switch happened when "it was called to Producer [Lee] Marcus' attention that Quinn is one of the very few Latin-American actors of any prominence in Hollywood and it would not be conducive to inter-American amity to have him as such a despicable character."

For a while it appeared that Kent Taylor, a screen veteran, would

> "The fugitives failed to present themselves for registration under the Selective Service law, and draft dodging was a federal offense.

Roger Touhy, Gangster: The Movie

Just 65 minutes long, *Roger Touhy, Gangster* (1944) begins like . . . well, like gangbusters. After scrolling text absolves the FBI of any blame or credit for what's to follow—and thanks the governor of Illinois and the Joliet prison's warden for their support in the film's making—the screen erupts in a 45-second montage of machine-gun bullets, bombs, and screeching black sedans. The images recall the prewar heyday of gangster films, many made at Warner Bros., where Bryan Foy ran the B unit in the 1930s. Now at 20th Century Fox, Foy intended *Roger Touhy, Gangster* to deliver a new level of realism to crime pictures. As one critic wrote, the film was "a new type of gangster picture, an unadorned film biography of a public enemy." James Agee noted, however, that "*Touhy* has some fairly exciting and intelligent things in it, and anyone who loves the best of the old gangster films will get some nostalgic pleasure out of it; but it is a long way short even of the ordinary ones in immediacy, drive, tension, and imagination."

Foy had planned to cast Lloyd Nolan, Anthony Quinn, Preston Foster, and Reed Hadley, all from the roster of his last picture, *Guadalcanal Diary* (1943). But Nolan balked and Foster, who'd played a humble and heroic priest in *Guadalcanal Diary*, ended up with the lead role. He portrays Touhy as uneducated, violent, superstitious, and humorless. If it was Foy's purpose, in support of his own Chicago mob cronies, to drain any redeeming qualities from the gangster's reputation, the film is an unqualified success. The only levity comes from character actor Frank "Off-the-Cuff" Jenks, who plays Touhy gang member "Troubles" O'Connor. Cy Kendall brings a strange edginess to his uncredited role as the partner of Touhy's kidnap victim, Joe Sutton, who is played with no energy and little imagination by William Post Jr. By contrast, Group Theatre veteran Henry Morgan, in the cheap-creep mode common in some of his earliest roles, delivers the goods as the gang's traitor, "Smoke" Reardon, who helps send his fellow "Touhy Terribles" up the river. Eight years after testifying against Touhy, Smoke finds himself in Stateville Prison with the rest of the gang ("I guess you guys are pretty sore"). When the terrified stool pigeon gets killed (offscreen, surprisingly), Touhy loses his last best chance of having his conviction overturned—and so the prison break is put in motion.

As Touhy's right-hand man "The Owl" Banghart, Victor McLaglen is hard to buy as a former teacher obsessed with correcting everyone's grammar. One critic described it as "an inverse comedy technique of speaking Oxonian English through his battered nose." Director Robert Florey had made experimental films in the 1920s, some with famed master of montage, Slavko Vorkapich. Here, he goes montage-mad from the start, filling what seems like a third of the film with quick-cut edits to display the end of Prohibition and the daily life of the prison population. Much is made out of the location shots of the actual prison—a novelty at the time—but frequent use of rear projection proves distracting and awkward.

For its time, *Roger Touhy, Gangster* was noteworthy for trying to deromanticize the gangster hero and bring more realism to the genre. One critic wrote, "The picture is presented in straightforward reportorial style, which gives the authority of a documentary film." But, like the "hangdog surrender" the fugitives make to the feds at the film's end, the movie deflates—giving in to moralizing speeches from Stateville's actual warden about the wages of sin. For this one, Bryan Foy, famed King of Bs, deserves a B grade, at best.

—*John Wranovics*

Preston Foster portrayed Roger Touhy with what the great film critic Manny Farber described as "ever reliable surliness."

ROGER TOUHY, GANGSTER!

Preston FOSTER ~ Victor McLAGLEN ~ Lois ANDREWS ~ Kent TAYLOR

20th CENTURY-FOX PICTURE

DIRECTED BY ROBERT FLOREY
PRODUCED BY LEE MARCUS

get the title role in what was now being called *Roger Touhy, Last of the Gangsters*. Unfortunately for Taylor, he had to trade roles with Foster, since the close-cropped haircut Taylor had adopted for his previous role as a Nazi agent hadn't grown out.

Original director Eugene Forde was replaced by Robert Florey, who'd previously worked for Foy on *Dangerously They Live* (1941) and *Lady Gangster* (1942). Florey and Foy were given unprecedented access to Stateville Prison. "Foy and Director Robert Florey not only got to photograph the state penitentiary and many of its 5,000 inmates," noted a news item, "but even the prison garbage truck and the ladder used by the Touhy gang in their sensational jail break last October." Florey later noted that the film's shooting schedule ran an extra two weeks "on account of all the searching. One day I was searched sixteen times. It took me two hours once to get permission to walk through one door. And many of the prisoners refused to show their faces to the camera. It was a very depressing experience."

Touhy went to court to fight against the film's release. On August 4, 1943, he won an injunction preventing 20th Century Fox from advertising or exhibiting the movie. A couple of days later, the injunction was lifted on the grounds that Touhy "had not contended that the film portrayed him falsely." Touhy filed an amended injunction, which was quickly rejected by the court.

The FBI also stalled the film's release, protesting that the movie gave undue credit to local law enforcement when the plaudits properly belonged to the bureau. The FBI demanded that the studio reshoot parts of the film. An article in February 1944 reported, "*Roger Touhy, Gangster* . . . made nearly a year ago, is still . . . on the shelf at 20th Century-Fox. Not only does Touhy, in prison at Joliet, Ill., threaten an injunction preventing its showing, but the FBI has objected to the way its agents acted in the run-down. Bryan Foy, producer, just returned from an FBI conference in Washington, plans to shoot some added scenes."

The completed film, had its premiere at Stateville Prison on July 12, 1944. Touhy refused to watch it, opting to remain in his cell. Also skipping the show was John "Jake the Barber" Factor, renamed Joe Sutton in the movie. Factor had just begun a ten-year sentence for mail fraud, having been convicted of reselling bonded whiskey certificates. The premiere (which included over a thousand invited guests) suffered setbacks when Touhy's compatriots cut the power supply to the speakers and radiator valves were pried opened to feed steam into the sweltering auditorium. Showtime was delayed by almost 90 minutes.

The film received positive reviews when it appeared in theaters that summer. But Touhy's family was ultimately successful in stanching its circulation, settling a lawsuit for defamation against Fox and Chicago's Balaban and Katz Theater Corporation, suing each for $500,000. Touhy settled for $15,000 and the understanding that 20th Century Fox would destroy the film and never distribute it again in the United States.

In 1954, Touhy succeeded in getting US district judge John P. Barnes to rule that John Factor had faked his own kidnapping. Barnes's decision was overruled by an appeals court, but in 1959, after serving more than twenty-five years for a kidnapping he always maintained had been a set-up, Touhy—now sixty-one—was released from Stateville. Twenty-three days later, on December 16, 1959, he was shotgunned to death on the porch of his sister's home.

Jake the Barber was released from prison in 1949. By 1955, he and his wife, Rella, were in charge of the Stardust Hotel in Las Vegas, which was secretly controlled by Chicago mob bosses Paul Ricca, Tony Accardo, Murray Humphreys, and Sam Giancana. Foy's good buddy Johnny Roselli would later tell LA-based mobster Jimmy Fratianno, "I got the Stardust for Chicago." During Factor's tenure at the hotel-casino, from 1955–63, the Justice Department estimated that the Chicago outfit skimmed between $48–200 million dollars from the Stardust alone.

By the mid-1970s, *Roger Touhy, Gangster* was starting to regularly appear on television; Touhy's estate sued CBS, Fox, and Balaban and Katz for breach of contract. The estate alleged that under the provisions of the settlement reached in 1949, "Twentieth Century-Fox had agreed that the film was never to be shown within the

In Chicago to sue Touhy for libel, Factor—informed of the gangster's murder—said, "This really breaks me up. I just hope they find the killer."

U.S. but was to be destroyed." In 1979, the court ruled against the Touhy estate.

John Factor's final years were spent rehabilitating his reputation as a "noted philanthropist" who spent his fortune on a wide range of charities. When he died in 1984, at age ninety-one, four hundred people attended his funeral. California governor Edmund G. "Pat" Brown and Los Angeles mayor Tom Bradley gave eulogies.

In the early 1960s, confronted by a *Los Angeles Times* reporter probing his criminal history, Jake the Barber had wept, asking, "How much does a man have to do to bury his past?" His remains now reside in the Hollywood Forever Cemetery. ∎

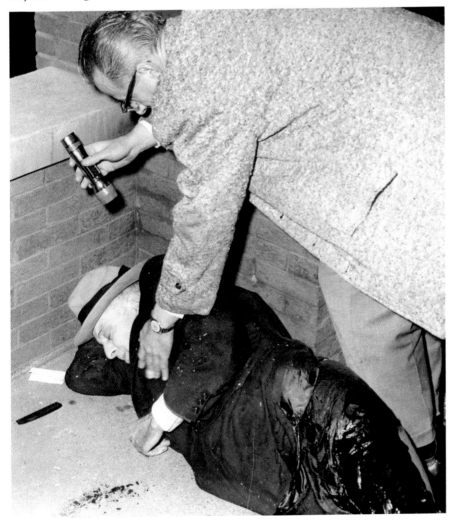

On December 16, 1959, free for less than a month, Touhy was shotgunned on his sister's porch in Chicago. He'd contended that the Factor kidnapping was a hoax until the very end.

RIPPED FROM THE HEADLINES!

Starting in 1934, strict enforcement of the Motion Picture Production Code mandated that moviemakers steer clear of stories based on actual crimes. Concern over "glorification" of criminal behavior began to dissipate, however, during the film noir movement. **EDDIE MULLER** offers a selective survey of significant fact-based noirs that paved the way for today's abundance of true crime tales.

Dillinger (1945)

Hollywood's bosses made a pact in 1935 to not produce films about actual outlaws—especially John Dillinger, whose Robin Hood persona captured the public's imagination during the Depression. The King Brothers thumbed their noses at that edict ten years later with this down-and-dirty depiction of Dillinger's exploits. Phil Yordan's Oscar-nominated script took a just-the-facts approach, eschewing moralizing. Though the film was mostly cobbled together from stock footage (one robbery is lifted from 1937's *You Only Live Once*), Lawrence Tierney's malevolent performance as Public Enemy #1 made *Dillinger* a smash. Veteran director Frank Borzage, however, excoriated the film and public guardians demanded the prints be destroyed. The Kings laughed all the way to the bank—yet it would be more than a decade before Dillinger reappeared onscreen, played by Leo Gordon in 1957's *Baby Face Nelson* (with Mickey Rooney in the title role), part of a pent-up wave of late 1950s gangster bios that included *The Scarface Mob* (1959), *Al Capone* (1959), *The Rise and Fall of Legs Diamond* (1960), and *Murder, Inc.* (1960).

Boomerang! (1947)

The safer strategy for true crime adaptations in postwar Hollywood was to focus on do-gooders righting miscarriages of justice. 20th Century Fox chief Darryl Zanuck, with producer Louis de Rochemont, pioneered the "semi-documentary" approach to crime with *The House on 92nd Street* (1945), conjoining actual FBI cases of home-front espionage. *Boomerang!*, made two years later, was based on the 1924 case of Harold Israel, a vagrant accused of murdering Catholic priest Hubert Dahme in Bridgeport, Connecticut.

Richard Murphy's Oscar-nominated screenplay described the political pressure brought on skeptical prosecutor Henry Harvey (Dana Andrews), who was expected to win a fast conviction. Opposition in Bridgeport to the story's retelling forced location shooting to nearby Stamford. The film is notable for *not* solving the crime—the DA ends up intentionally exonerating the suspect he's supposed to convict. The actual case remains unsolved. The real-life prosecutor, Homer Cummings, gained sufficient notoriety to become a player in Democratic party politics and in 1933 was appointed attorney general by President Roosevelt. 20th Century Fox followed the success of *Boomerang!* with *Call Northside 777* (1948), another semi-documentary retelling of a real-life crime (learn more about that case and film in Imogen Sara Smith's article, pg. 8).

Canon City (1948)

The breakout of twelve convicts from the federal prison in Canon (pronounced "canyon") City, Colorado, on December 30, 1947, gave writer-director Crane Wilbur inspiration for yet another prison yarn. Wilbur, "the Potentate of Prison Pictures," had been writing men-behind-bars sagas since the 1930s. What made this one historically significant is that it was done in partnership with Eagle-Lion producer Bryan Foy and "silent partner" Johnny Roselli, the Chicago mob's man in Hollywood. It starts as a faux documentary (Warden Roy Best playing himself) but soon becomes full-on noir—photographed by John Alton—with vignettes tracking the desperate fugitives. Poster art promised explosive violence, but the film is a hushed and sweaty affair. It kills a few cons for dramatic effect, but in actuality the escapees were all recaptured within the week. *LIFE* later ran a photo of them back in stir, watching *Canon City* on movie night. Jim Sherbondy, the reluctant escapee played by Scott Brady, remained in the state's penal system until 1969, when he was killed trying to escape from a prison work farm.

He Walked by Night (1948)

Bryan Foy, Crane Wilbur, and Johnny Roselli strike again. Wilbur developed the film from the real-life story of Erwin Walker, a war vet and police dispatcher who was a one-man crime wave in postwar Los Angeles, PTSD psychosis leading him on a yearlong

Richard Basehart gives a tour de force performance as Roy Martin, a psychotic loner based on the real-life Erwin Walker, whose actual story was far more complex than the movie based on his notorious Los Angeles crime spree. Scott Brady is the KO victim in this scene.

spree stealing weapons and electronics. It culminated in his killing highway patrolman Loren Roosevelt on June 5, 1946. In custody, Walker claimed he was inventing a ray gun that turned metal to dust, making it too costly to fight more wars. More interesting to Wilbur were the forensics of the manhunt and how Walker had used sewers to evade capture. Famously Jack Webb, who played a police lab technician, used the film as inspiration for his *Dragnet* radio and television shows. Walker was judged sane and sentenced to the gas chamber. Days before execution, Walker tried to hang himself; a psychiatrist declared him a "paranoid schizophrenic." Doctors worked to return his sanity—so the state could execute him. Instead, Walker became a model prisoner, and was paroled in 1974. He changed his name, worked as a chemist, and lived to be ninety-one.

The Undercover Man (1949)

While the FBI forbade films being made about Al Capone, Columbia circumvented that with *The Undercover Man*. It was based on Frank Wilson, the Treasury agent who brought down Capone for income tax evasion. Elmer Irey, who led the investigative team during Capone's prosecution, said that Wilson "fears nothing that walks. He will sit quietly looking at books eighteen hours a day, seven days a week—forever, if he wants to find something in those

books." Not even as kinetic a director as Joseph H. Lewis, nor an actor as charismatic as Glenn Ford, could put much life into such a by-the-book hero. Capone, renamed Salvatore Rocco (Anthony Caruso), is relegated to a supporting role, the story's focus sticking with the paper-chasing feds. It would be another ten years before Hollywood tried to tackle Capone's saga. Nicholas Ray's *Party Girl* (1958) had Lee J. Cobb's Rico Angelo as a Capone surrogate. *The Scarface Mob* (1959) pitted Eliot Ness (Robert Stack) against Capone (Neville Brand), and Rod Steiger chewed all available scenery as *Al Capone* (1959), which told the tale from his POV—a no-no ten years earlier.

Lonely Heart Bandits (1950)

This obscure Republic B is a historical footnote for being the first film based on the notorious exploits of serial killers Ray Fernandez and Martha Beck. Between 1947 and 1949, the pair, pretending to be brother and sister, preyed on women who placed "lonely heart" ads in newspapers. They were arrested March 1, 1949, and although suspected of as many as seventeen murders, were tried only for the murder of sixty-six-year-old Janet Fay. Fernandez and Beck were executed in Sing Sing on March 8, 1951, six months after the release of *Lonely Heart Bandits*.  The 60-minute B, directed by George Blair and starring John Eldredge and Dorothy Patrick as the renamed killer-lovers, is a sanitized version of the gruesome reality, which never could have been depicted in the Code-dominated era. Once the PCA was dead, however, the tale was resurrected many times: *The Honeymoon Killers* (1970), *Deep Crimson* (Mexico, 1996), *Lonely Hearts* (2006), and *Alleluia* (Belgium, 2014) are all imaginative and bloody interpretations of the story.

Highway 301 (1950)

By 1950, Bryan Foy was back at Warner Bros., where in the 1930s he ran the studio's B unit. He found another true crime aficionado in writer-director Andrew Stone, who'd knocked around Hollywood since the silent era. Stone anticipated the rise of independent films and knew crime stories offered good return on investment in a system starting to crack apart. He pitched Foy a yarn from a file of 1,500 true crime cases he'd collected. The result was a brutal depiction of the Tri-State Gang, who in 1934 robbed and killed

their way through Pennsylvania, Maryland, and Virginia. Leader Walter Legenza (Steve Cochran) briefly nudged Dillinger from the top of the FBI's "Most Wanted" list. The film takes viewers hostage on a crime spree that turns shockingly violent. The real Legenza was arrested in 1934, convicted, and sentenced to death. Weeks before execution, he had guns smuggled into the jail in a canned chicken. He and cohort Robert Mais shot their way out, rampaging for another three months. Once recaptured, they were electrocuted within the week.

Try and Get Me! (1951)

In 1933, Harold Thurmond and Jack Holmes kidnapped Brooke Hart, scion of a San Jose mercantile family. They demanded $40,000 for his return—although Hart had already been drowned. Captured, Thurmond and Holmes blamed each other for Hart's "accident," leading the press to speculate on a possible mistrial, or an acquittal for one of the men. Riled up by the speculation, citizens descended on the jail. The sheriff begged Governor James Rolph to have the National Guard keep the peace. Rolph refused. The mob overran the cops, dragged Thurmond and Holmes from their cells, and hanged them in the town square. Rolph praised the mob for saving taxpayers the trouble. Producer Robert Stillman bought *The Condemned*, Jo Pagano's 1947 novel about the incident, because of parallels between mob lynching and current anti-Communist hysteria. Director Cy Endfield, soon blacklisted himself, kept an intense focus on the Thurmond character, renamed Howard Tyler (Frank Lovejoy), making this tale of a desperate man's spiral into hell perhaps the bleakest noir ever.

Fourteen Hours (1951)

On July 26, 1938, John Warde brought downtown Manhattan to a standstill as he perched on the seventeenth-floor ledge of the Gotham Hotel, threatening to jump. The first officer at the scene, Charles Glasco, consoled the young man for fourteen hours, but couldn't save him; Warde leapt (or fell) to his death. In the film version (written by John Paxton, directed by Henry Hathaway), suicidal Robert Cosick (Richard Basehart) teeters on the ledge as a callous city gawks. Despite the efforts of Officer Dunnigan (Paul Douglas) to talk him down, Cosick falls to his death. In the last shot, a

sanitation truck washes away his splattered remains. At least that's what audiences saw at the film's premiere. That same day in New York, the daughter of 20th Century Fox president Spyros Skouras killed herself by leaping from her room in Bellevue Hospital. Devastated, Skouras ordered *Fourteen Hours* pulled from theaters. Darryl Zanuck saved the studio's investment, rounding up a few actors and a skeleton crew (Basehart not among them) and shooting a new ending in which Cosick is whisked to safety.

I Was a Communist for the FBI (1951)

The Communist witch hunt required at least one "true crime" exposé. Again, Foy and Wilbur leapt into the breach, creating a Cold War curio based on Matt Cvetic, an FBI agent who infiltrated the Pittsburgh chapter of the Communist Party of the United States. By 1947, the FBI doubted Cvetic's reliability, due to arrests for disorderly behavior. But Cvetic parlayed his undercover stint into a popular radio show, and Foy bought the rights for Warner Bros. Frank Lovejoy starred in Wilbur's largely fictionalized story. In a move both unforgivable and inexplicable, the Academy nominated *I Was a Communist for the FBI* as Best Documentary of 1951. By then Cvetic had grown increasingly erratic and the FBI severed all connections with him. He lost a bid for a Republican senate seat in 1954, and the next year his son had him committed for electroshock therapy. Upon release Cvetic joined the John Birch Society and other right-wing, Christian-based crusades. He died of a heart attack while waiting in line for a driver's license at the Los Angeles DMV.

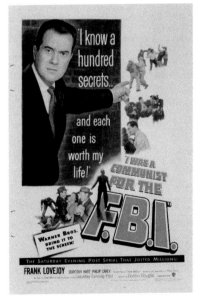

The Captive City (1952)

A landmark in the changing economics and techniques of American moviemaking. Robert Wise and Mark Robson, both editors turned directors, formed Aspen Pictures to make modest movies of their own choice—and keep the profits. Their maiden effort was inspired by the US Senate's Special Committee to Investigate Organized Crime, which captivated the United States in 1951 with its televised hearings. Chaired by Democrat Estes Kefauver, it exposed organized crime's inroads into American society. Wise hired journalist Alvin Josephy Jr., veteran investigator of the rackets, to turn his experiences into a tale about a reporter (John Forsythe) exposing a small-town crime cabal. It was shot on location in Reno, using many amateur actors. Kefauver, launching a presidential bid, appeared in an onscreen prologue and epilogue. When he unexpectedly won the New Hampshire Democratic primary, incumbent president Harry Truman was forced from the race. Despite its timeliness, *The Captive City* lost money. Films copying its exposé style with bigger stars, like *The Turning Point* (1952), fared better. In Hollywood, it rarely pays to be first.

The Hitch-Hiker (1953)

Billy Cook was a petty thief whose miserable life led to a Southwest crime spree in 1950, during which he killed a traveling salesman and a family of five. *The Hitch–Hiker*, produced and directed by Ida Lupino, is based on the ordeal of James Burke and Forrest Damron, who survived an eight-day nightmare when they picked up Cook during a fishing trip in Mexico. Lupino got the hostages' story firsthand, and visited the convicted killer in San Quentin, on death row. She wanted Cook to okay the use of his name in the film. The FBI nixed it, arguing that criminals should not profit from their acts—be it through money or notoriety. Lupino and husband/coproducer, Collier Young, wrote the script, and she got career-best work from Edmond O'Brien and Frank Lovejoy as the hostages and William Talman as Cook, renamed "Emmett Myers." Despite the names being changed, many factual details remained—including the deformity that kept "Cockeyed" Cook's right eye from closing, one of the more unnerving aspects of the film. Cook, twenty-three, was executed in the gas chamber on December 12, 1952.

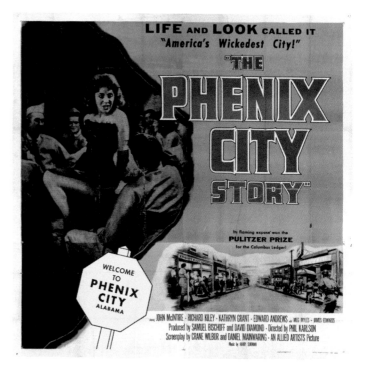

The Phenix City Story (1955)

During World War II, Phenix City, Alabama (pop. 24,000), earned an outsized reputation as a den of iniquity. City fathers offered no resistance to the racket-run gambling and prostitution that became the town's economic engine. That changed on June 14, 1954, when Albert Patterson, a local lawyer who won the Democratic primary for attorney general by vowing to clean up the city, was murdered. Crane Wilbur—*who else?*—swooped in to turn Patterson's murder into a project for producer Sam Bischoff. On-location production was entrusted to Phil Karlson, who arrived in Phenix City only weeks after Patterson's death, with the killers still at large. He brazenly took cameras into the notorious 14th Street district—a haven for racketeers—and enticed locals to appear, giving the film unnerving verisimilitude. In his zeal for authenticity, Karlson dressed actor John McIntire in the actual suit Patterson was wearing when he was shot to death. Eventually a grand jury handed down 734 indictments against Phenix City cops, elected officials, and business owners who'd catered to organized crime.

The Night Holds Terror (1955)

The mid-1950s saw many home invasion hostage dramas, including *Suddenly* (1954), *Storm Fear* (1955), *The Desperate Hours* (1955),

Pressbook cover for *The Captive City*, exploiting the film's many real-life connections.

and this low-budget thriller. The main factors were Cold War–inspired insecurity that we weren't safe in our own homes, coupled with a rise in juvenile delinquency, exploited in movies like *The Wild One* (1953) and *Blackboard Jungle* (1955). *The Night Holds Terror* depicts an actual 1953 incident in Lancaster, California—which also inspired *The Desperate Hours*. But this was no William Wyler show—Andrew and Virginia Stone, applying their now-patented formula, ditched the studio sets in favor of shooting *everything* on location, where events actually occurred. Gone was the classic noir look, replaced by natural sound and lighting. The Stones paid survivors Gene and Dorothy Courtier $500 for the use of their names—an idea that backfired when two of the convicted perps brought lawsuits, contending: 1) they too should have been paid, and 2) the movie ruined any hope for their rehabilitation after parole. Gene Courtier punched out one of his kidnappers in front of the jury. The judge dismissed the case—and the convicts' call for a mistrial.

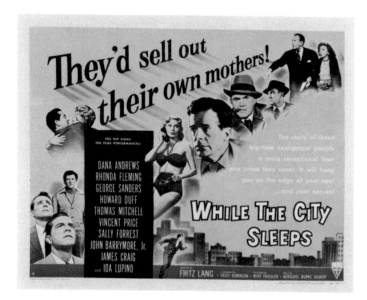

While the City Sleeps (1956)

The 1953 novel *The Bloody Spur* appealed to Fritz Lang because it had echoes of his masterpiece *M* (1931). Both were based on a true crime. Between 1945 and 1946, Chicago had been terrorized by the murders of several young women. The culprit used a victim's lipstick to scrawl a plea for his capture at one murder scene. As the manhunt for the "Lipstick Killer" led nowhere, newspapers spurred the public's bloody imaginings. Hence the novel, by Chicago reporter Charles Einstein. Lang loved its mordant cynicism; reporters backstabbing each other in pursuit of the killer—not because they want justice, but because whoever nabs the killer wins a promotion. The accused "Lipstick Killer" was seventeen-year-old William Heirens, a student at the University of Chicago who dabbled in burglary. After he was arrested near the site of one killing, police claimed his fingerprints matched those found on a note in one victim's home. Pre-Miranda, Heirens was beaten by cops and injected with "truth serum" until he confessed to one of the killings. He was charged with all three "Lipstick" murders and, on advice of lawyers, pled guilty on the promise of a life sentence instead of the chair. "I lied so I could live," he cried to the press. Case reviews were denied multiple times, and Heirens lived the rest of his life in prison. He died in 2012, at age eighty-three, maintaining his innocence to the end.

The Wrong Man (1956)

On January 14, 1953, Manny Balestrero, headed home from a regular gig at Manhattan's Stork Club, was braced by police, as he fit the description of a robbery suspect. So began his descent into the New York justice system. *The Wrong Man*, starring Henry Fonda as Balestrero, is the only Alfred Hitchcock movie closely based on a true story. (See the review of *Nothing to Fear*, a new book about the movie and the case, on pg. 74.) In contrast to his usual style, the director went all-in for authenticity, shooting where the actual story took place, which included the cell where Manny was held and the sanitarium where his distraught wife, Rose (Vera Miles), was committed. Critics were largely dismissive, some even accusing the director of altering facts. What critics really missed was Hitchcock's usual humor. The director could usually be counted on for amusing business around the suspense, but *The Wrong Man* is unrelentingly grim. Hitchcock was angered by Warner Bros.'s insistence on a coda assuring viewers that Rose Balestrero regained her sanity. She did not. Manny sued for false arrest, getting $7,000 of the $50,000 he sought. The $22,000 Warner paid for his story all went to Rose's medical care.

I Want to Live! (1958)

A Pulitzer Prize–winning series of articles by *San Francisco Examiner* reporter Ed Montgomery provided the framework for this sensational account of the life of Barbara Graham, who on June 3, 1955, became the last woman executed in California. Graham was con-

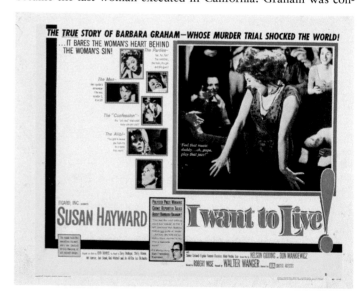

Henry Fonda gave a compelling—if enervatingly passive—performance as Manny Balestrero in Alfred Hitchcock's 1956 noir-verité drama *The Wrong Man*.

victed as an accomplice in the robbery/murder of Mabel Monohan, but in jailhouse interviews with Montgomery she claimed to have been duped into it by shady cohorts. She felt her life as a hard-partying prostitute—readily related to the sympathetic reporter—prevented a fair trial. Producer Walter Wanger—who'd served time himself for wounding romantic rival Jennings Lang—hired a stellar team to tell Graham's tawdry tale. Robert Wise juiced up vestiges of his *Captive City* docudrama approach with a propulsive Johnny Mandel jazz score and a fiery performance from Susan Hayward, who'd win the Oscar for her portrayal of Graham. All previous films about capital punishment looked away from the actual execution, but *I Want to Live!* showed it in excruciating detail, making it a landmark film for that reason alone.

In Cold Blood (1967)

The best-selling book of 1966 related the November 15, 1959, murders of the Clutter family in Holcomb, Kansas, a "senseless" crime

Scott Wilson and Robert Blake brought a new level of unnerving realism to their roles as disaffected killers in the stunning film version of Truman Capote's true crime classic *In Cold Blood.*

TRUMAN CAPOTE'S
IN COLD BLOOD

Written for the screen and directed by RICHARD BROOKS
Music by QUINCY JONES / A COLUMBIA PICTURES RELEASE / PANAVISION®

Positively no one under 16 admitted unless accompanied by a parent or guardian. [M.A.]

no one in the bucolic region could comprehend. The trauma would have remained localized if not for the arrival of two out-of-towners: Truman Capote and his colleague Harper Lee, already working on the novel *To Kill a Mockingbird* (1960), which would earn her lasting fame. Before the suspects were apprehended, Capote and Lee interviewed dozens of townsfolk and law enforcement, capturing a mosaic of Midwestern small-town life. Once killers Perry Smith and Dick Hickock were in custody, Capote had almost exclusive access to them. The resulting book (six years in the writing) was groundbreaking, not just for its novelistic approach to a true crime but for probing the lives of the killers as well as the victims. Director Richard Brooks, who also wrote the screenplay, filmed where events actually occurred—including the murder house. Conrad Hall's stunning black-and-white cinematography mixed frigid verité footage with dramatically lit scenes that played like the ghosts of film noirs past. The presence of veteran actors Paul Stewart and Charles McGraw added further reverberations of old-school noir, but Scott Wilson and Robert Blake, as Hickock and Smith (both hanged), brought a despairing depth and urgency to true crime movies never before seen. Unflinching and uncompromised, both book and film revolutionized the way such stories were told, making painful, heartbreaking "sense" of a random murder. The film culminated a year of massive change in American cinema—*Bonnie and Clyde*, *The Graduate*, *Guess Who's Coming to Dinner*, and *In the Heat of the Night* were all nominated for Best Picture—but Hollywood's old guard, desperately clinging to its reliance on reassuring entertainments, chose *Dr. Doolittle* instead of *In Cold Blood* for the final Best Picture nomination. There's no doubt, however, which film had the bigger impact on American culture. For proof, just browse any contemporary source that streams podcasts and movies. ∎

REEL WEST

BLOOD ON
THE MOON   ALAN K. RODE

"A first-rate look at an undervalued movie that represents a noted Western author (Luke Short), a talented screenwriter (Lillie Hayward), a director who was just coming into his own (Robert Wise), and a star on the ascendance (Robert Mitchum). Alan K. Rode gives us the story behind the story onscreen."

—LEONARD MALTIN, author of *Leonard Maltin's Classic Movie Guide*

Available in paperback and e-book

UNIVERSITY OF NEW MEXICO PRESS

unmpress.com

IN HARM'S WAY

By Vance
McLaughlin

The Real-Life Killer Who Inspired *The Night of the Hunter*

Preacher Harry Powell (Robert Mitchum) is one of Hollywood's most iconic and extreme depictions of evil. Everybody knows who he is, whether you've watched Charles Laughton's *The Night of the Hunter* (1955) a dozen times or merely stumbled upon an image of the false preacher with the words "love" and "hate" tattooed across his knuckles. Powell is so unrelentingly sinister, and so outsize in the presentation of his deadly grift, that it's difficult to imagine him existing outside of the film's exaggerated Gothic setting. He's the foundation upon which children's nightmares are built. What many don't realize, however, is that the character is based on a real person.

The Night of the Hunter was adapted from the 1953 novel of the same name by Davis Grubb, which was inspired by the exploits of serial killer Harry F. Powers. At least, that was the name he was using when he got caught. Powers, born Harm Drenth, adopted a number of aliases during his Depression-era crime spree that consisted of extortion, theft, and the murder of five people. There are unmistakable parallels with Preacher Powell, but the further one wades into the real-life story, the more it becomes clear that Powers was even more twisted than his fictional counterpart.

Powers emigrated from Holland to the United States in 1910, when he was seventeen. He'd developed a reputation for lying and stealing at an early age, and his parents sent him abroad with another family, hopeful that he would land work on a farm and develop a sense of independence. The agriculture work didn't take but the independence did— albeit in ways in which the elder Drenths would not have approved. Powers boosted a car from a Wisconsin senator in 1919, and broke out of jail before the auto theft could be brought to trial. It was his 1921 arrest, however, that proved the most formative in terms of his future modus operandi.

Powers became obsessed with a twenty-year-old woman named Rose Strickland, and when she decided to marry someone else he broke into the newlyweds' home, found her wedding gown, and ripped it apart. He then tried to ransack the house and burn it to the ground. Never mind the fact that Powers had no romantic history with Strickland; from his compromised perspective, he had been led on and betrayed, so whatever heinous acts he committed should be excused as "justifiable." Powers was convicted of burglary and sentenced to eighteen months in a Wisconsin state prison. Upon release, he discovered a profitable way to align his misogyny with his criminal impulses. He called it the "widow racket."

By 1924, Powers was regularly bilking desperate women out of their money. He became so good at the widow racket, in fact, that he eventually convinced marks to run away with him under the false promise of marriage. The risk increased over time, but so did the

Powers (above) differed from his fictional counterpart (right) in presentation, but both men were willing to harm women and children for monetary gain.

Police were forced to relocate Powers after a lynch mob formed outside his jail cell. The incident was dramatized in *The Night of the Hunter*.

reward. Powers stole one woman's car and valuables during a seemingly innocuous stop at a gas station restroom. In another instance, Powers doctored a St. Louis widow's coffee with sleeping powder then rummaged through her home, stealing all her valuables.

Powers juggled numerous marks simultaneously, placing advertisements in matrimonial agency magazines as a way of attracting potential victims. He honed his skills, polished his ad, and kept up correspondence with numerous women who met his criterion. Powers developed a code he'd write on letters received from future victims, so he could remember the particular stage of his courtship with each of his applicants. If any reply to his letters raised a red flag, he stopped writing. He kept notebooks filled with phrases appropriated from literature, poems, and popular magazines, which he'd include in his missives to convince women of his honesty and ardor. Most of the victims Powers attracted during the Depression were so terrified of destitution and loneliness that they discarded their gut instinct or rational doubts about their suitor.

While Powers saw himself as a seducer of women in the mold of his idol, Rudolph Valentino, he was in reality what one jailer described as "pudgy with a fat face." He created a persona based on stylish clothing, flashy vehicles, and the illusion of worldliness.

This charade paid off when Powers met Luella "Lulu" Strother, a divorcée in Clarksburg, West Virginia. The two connected through one of Powers's matrimonial ads, where Lulu revealed that she and her sister Belle lived with an ailing mother, and were set to inherit

> "Most of the victims Powers attracted during the Depression were so terrified of destitution and loneliness that they discarded their gut instinct or rational doubts about their suitor.

Powers in Clarksburg, West Virginia, when he confessed to killing Asta Eicher. His trial drew so many spectators that it was held at a nearby opera house.

a store and a piece of farmland when their mother passed. Powers married Strother in 1927, moving into the family home adjacent to the store. It was a perfect arrangement, providing a base of operations, a person to care for him, and a meager but steady income beyond his own illegal earnings.

Powers's sense of security once again emboldened his criminal escapades. He had a garage built onto the Strother property, and a basement containing four rooms modified with soundproof tiles, heavy doors with locks, and a drain. He determined that holding his female victims captive would make the extortion process easier, and when he was done he could simply kill them and dispose of the evidence. Asta Eicher was the first woman to meet this cruel fate. She was picked up by Powers on June 25, 1931, and was so eager to elope that she agreed to leave her three children with a housekeeper. Powers soon discovered that Eicher was in debt, however, and her Illinois home was nearing foreclosure, so he was forced to travel to the Prairie State on multiple occasions to sell furniture and cover mortgage payments. After failed attempts to cash checks with Eicher's forged signature, Powers decided he'd had enough. He killed Eicher and her children, and told concerned Illinois neighbors that the family had simply taken a trip to Europe.

A month after Eicher's ill-fated elopement, Massachusetts divorcee Dorothy Lemke disappeared under similar circumstances. Powers later revealed plans to murder at least five more victims, including his sister-in-law and his wife (whose awareness of, and involvement in her husband's crimes was never made entirely clear). Fortunately, he left a trail of clues in his wake. In August 1931, police were able to trace Eicher's love letters and a stolen license plate back to Powers, despite the fact that he had been using the alias "Pierson." They searched the killer's basement and discovered five corpses, including those of Eicher and Lemke, who had both been beaten beyond recognition and had their hair ripped out of their heads. Powers was

subjected to a beating of his own after his arrest, and was told that if he didn't admit his guilt he would be turned over to the local townspeople. He acquiesced, and was promptly sentenced to be hanged.

In the novel *The Night of the Hunter*, Davis Grubb used Powers's crimes, primarily those involving the Eicher family, as fodder for his creative instincts. There are several liberties taken with the case, however, making it clear that the author intended to craft a compelling story rather than a factual retelling. The film adaptation opens with self-ordained preacher Harry Powell sharing a cell with Ben Harper (Peter Graves), a man who is to be hanged for killing two men in a bank robbery. Harper, talking in his sleep, gives Powell the notion that the doomed man's family might know where he hid the loot from the robbery. When Powell is released, he befriends Harper's widow, Willa (Shelley Winters), and they quickly marry. Willa doesn't know where the money is hidden, but her son, John (Billy Chapin), and daughter, Pearl (Sally Jane Bruce), do. Seeing Willa as an obstacle to retrieving the money, Powell slits her throat, puts her in his Model T, and sinks it to the bottom of the river.

The similarities between Powers and Powell are primarily psychological. Both the real person and the character share a deep-rooted misogyny, which the novel and film give religious overtones. Powell is shown having a playful, one-sided conversation with God in which he can't remember if he has killed six or twelve widows. To him all women are Eve, the eternal temptress, and he is merely doing the Lord's work. The abhorrence of sexuality is another commonality. As Willa prepares for the physical consummation of their nuptials, Powell becomes outraged that she'd think a "man of the cloth" would have carnal desires. During the Powers trial, the killer revealed that he never consummated his marriage with Lulu, either. It was this lack of interest, ironically, that convinced Powers's victims he was a man of strong moral fiber and did not view women merely as sex objects.

The physical is where these two killers differ. Powell's "love" and "hate" tattoos were inspired by a chance encounter that Grubb had with a man at a Philadelphia bar, and the character's attire—along with his compulsive use of a switchblade—are fabricated (albeit effective) flourishes. In one telling scene, Powell attends a lascivious burlesque; as the dancer gyrates, he snaps open the switchblade, which rips through his pocket. The line between sexual repression and aggression proves thinner than the lining of his coat. In another scene, Powell flicks open his knife to scare the prepubescent Pearl. When she tries to touch it, he angrily pulls it away, warning her that this would make him "very, very mad." Thankfully, the children in the film avoid the same fate as their offscreen counterparts.

The Night of the Hunter spends most of its running time putting a Gothic twist on a Mother Goose nursery rhyme. Director Laughton was fascinated by the relationship between the orphaned children and the spinster (Lillian Gish) who eventually becomes their protector. He wasn't trying to sketch a nuanced character study of Powell, let alone the killer that inspired him. He wanted to create a villain that would repulse and frighten his viewers. It's telling that the closest the film comes to faithfully recreating the Powers case is the lynch mob sequence. In real life, a group of angry citizens

> **" He achieved a sliver of the fame Valentino had amassed the decade prior. The difference, of course, is that people wept when Valentino died, and they cheered when it was Powers's turn.**

gathered outside of the jail where Powers was being held, and police were forced to escort him out the back door. Laughton, realizing the power of seeing an egotistical killer reduced to shambles, does the same thing with the fictional Powell. The character is last shown disheveled and paranoid in the back seat of a car, while the hangman jokes about his execution.

Powers's fate was a bit more dramatic. The killer was transferred to West Virginia State Penitentiary in Moundsville, and his trial was held at an opera house because the number of spectators was so large. The Camden *Courier-Post* covered the trial and subsequent hanging, which became a cause célèbre for locals. "Moundsville had taken on a holiday festival appearance in preparation for the execution of the man whose crimes startled the world," the paper read. "Outside the prison, a crowd gathered along the curbs. Automobiles were lined up for blocks." Powers plummeted through the gallows on March 18, 1932, and dangled for eleven minutes before being pronounced dead. He achieved a sliver of the fame Valentino had amassed the decade prior. The difference, of course, is that people wept when Valentino died, and they cheered when it was Powers's turn. The killer was thirty-eight years old.

It's fitting that a man who spent decades telling lies clammed up when asked if he had any final words. He'd grown so accustomed to hiding behind aliases and mirroring his victims that when it came time to access his own feelings, Powers came up empty-handed. The condemnation of false prophets is what ultimately threads the real-life case, the novel, and the film together. There have been countless men like Harry J. Powers since 1932, and there will be more down the line, but sooner or later their facades crack, and the depleted humanity at their core bleeds through. As long as we abide, and endure, they will get their just deserts. ∎

NOTE: The editors thank Preston Neal Jones for his assistance.

Powers was given the nickname "West Virginia Bluebeard" by the press, despite not being married to any of his victims.

DOG DAY AFTERNOON'S MANY REALITIES

By Rachel Walther

August 22, 1972: It's a muggy afternoon in Brooklyn, and three men are about to rob the Chase Manhattan Bank at the corner of Avenue P and East Third Street. They enter the lobby, wait until the last customer of the day leaves, and then things go sideways. The first man chickens out immediately and scampers off. The two remaining robbers empty the safe, only to discover that the massive take they'd anticipated isn't there. The police get tipped off, surround the bank, and now it's cops versus robber for the next twelve hours, with the bank workers held hostage. During the interminable wai one of the robbers asks to see his wife—when the police locate her, she turns out to be a tran woman. When news that one of the robbers is homosexual gets out the standoff becomes media circus, with TV cameras and onlookers flooding the neighborhood waiting for a glimps of this guy, a mercurial and charismatic young man who's clearly in over his head. By early th next morning the misadventure has concluded at Kennedy Airport, with one robber dead and the other on his way to jail.

A "simple" robbery goes sideways: John Wojtowicz in a standoff with local police.

When folks got wind of the fact that Wojtowicz was robbing the bank to get money for his wife's sex-change operation, a media circus ensued.

This is the story of both the real-life incident that occurred in 1972 and the plot of *Dog Day Afternoon*, the film based on those events that was released three years later. What brought about this strange episode in New York's history is a sensational story of transformation, rebellion, and memory; it has gone on to have a fifty-year afterlife, with both the film and the wild biography of the real-life robber, John Wojtowicz, remaining as compelling today as the when the story first broke.

John Wojtowicz was an average guy from Brooklyn, a straitlaced Goldwater Republican pursuing the American Dream: a wife, Carmen; two kids; saving for a house in the suburbs. His tour in Vietnam changed everything—intimate experiences in the service with other men switched on a dormant aspect of Wojtowicz's sexuality, and when he returned stateside he left Carmen, changed his politics, and began to explore the gay scene in the West Village. Wojtowicz was a strange, arrogant little guy who badgered and coaxed men into codependent relationships and campaigned doggedly for gay rights at the Gay Activist Alliance (GAA). In 1971 he met Ernest Aron, a transvestite who identified as a woman; their relationship was fraught with grievances and heated arguments, but they were committed enough to each other that when Wojtowicz proposed (despite still being married to Carmen) the two were married in November at a café in Greenwich Village. After the wedding Aron became increasingly miserable—she was desperate for sex change operation but couldn't afford one and was suicidal at the thought

of remaining a man. Wojtowicz initially rebuffed Aron's pleas—he preferred a partner who looked like a woman but had a man's equipment—but after Aron cut her wrists the following August and ended up in the hospital, Wojtowicz vowed to get the money for the operation somewhere. He had an idea.

Wojtowicz rounded up a few guys he knew casually from around the neighborhood: Sal Naturale and Bobby Westenberg. On August 22, they psyched themselves up for the robbery by watching *The Godfather* at a theater in Times Square. Al Pacino's steely confidence in the film's final scenes, as he assumes the role of head of the Corleone family, was a swagger that Wojtowicz would imitate in the hours ahead. After they arrived at the Chase Manhattan in Brooklyn, Westenberg dropped out immediately and ran off, and Wojtowicz and Naturale were left to carry out the heist. It was a failure: the bank only had about $38,000 in cash, a much smaller take than they'd expected. The bank manager covertly signaled to a colleague over the phone that a robbery was in progress; police surrounded the bank and the two men decided to hold the workers hostage, bartering for their safe passage out of the country in exchange for the return of the employees.

They hadn't planned on hostages and didn't know what to do with them. Wojtowicz let everyone use the bathroom and allowed them to call their loved ones to let them know they were okay. The workers munched on the complimentary customer lollipops to stave off hunger; Wojtowicz ordered food for everyone from the cops outside. Folks started calling in to the bank—local law enforcement trying to ascertain the robbers' state of mind, psychos imploring Wojtowicz to "Kill them all!," and journalists eager to learn as much as possible about the situation. When asked by a reporter why he was robbing the bank, Wojtowicz explained that he needed the money to get his wife a sex-change operation, calmly stating,

Chris Sarandon (right) made his film debut as Leon, Ernest Aron's (left) fictional counterpart. His heartrending and humorous performance garnered him an Academy Award nomination for Best Supporting Actor.

"[My wife's] a guy. I'm gay."

When the media got wind of this, what seemed like a "simple" bank robbery story became a cause célèbre. Networks cut in on coverage of the Republican National Convention's nomination of Richard Nixon for reelection to hover around Avenue P and Third Street, hoping to get a glimpse of Wojtowicz as he stepped outside to negotiate with the cops and to hear more about his (to many, unknown) lifestyle. Hundreds mobbed the intersection—some to jeer at the criminals but mostly to cheer on the would-be bandits and boo at the cops. At 3 a.m. the show was on the road: the FBI had secured a jet for the two men, and they rode with a handful of remaining hostages to JFK. On the tarmac, in a lightning-fast confrontation Naturale was shot by the FBI and Wojtowicz was taken into custody. For the hostages, their nightmare was over—for Wojtowicz, a new reality was just beginning.

LIFE magazine ran a feature on the incident next month, recounting the "bizarre" details of Wojtowicz's marriage to Aron as well as focusing on the hapless but relatively humane treatment the two men provided to their captives and the Us versus Them attitude that spread out from the bank and onto the televisions of the East Coast: "After all, the robbers and the hostages are in this together, but the determined men outside are strangers."

"It took on its own life." — Al Pacino

Martin Bregman was a talent agent who aspired to produce motion pictures. He read "The Boys in the Bank" and saw potential, a project that he could develop and build around his star client, Al Pacino. He enlisted Frank Pierson, who'd scripted *Cool Hand Luke* (1967), to write the screenplay, and tasked Sidney Lumet to direct. After several unsuccessful attempts to meet with Wojtowicz in prison, Pierson opted instead to fashion an image of his main character, renamed Sonny Wortzik, based on interviews with anyone and everyone Wojtowicz had come in contact with. The more he spoke to people, the blurrier Pierson's notion of Wojtowicz became: "Everyone knew a different person and described a different person." To Carmen, John

was the model husband—a good provider and affectionate father; to Ernest Aron, he was volatile and dangerous; to the Brooklyn crowd on August 22, he was a charming ringleader. The one common thread for the screenwriter among all these disparate reports was Wojtowicz's desire to take care of everyone, to be who others needed him to be. It was this trait that he used to build Sonny, a sympathetic loser in over his head with the number of responsibilities he's saddled himself with, on the verge of snapping under the strain of managing the endless needs of his loved ones.

Pacino initially balked at the project. He was exhausted from months of nonstop shooting on *The Godfather Part II* (1974) and remembered that working with Lumet the year before on *Serpico* (1973) was rewarding but arduous. And, as the director would reflect years later: "No major American star that I know of had ever played a role like this." *Dog Day Afternoon* would be pushing the envelope, the first mainstream film to center around a gay character since the film adaptation of the successful 1968 play *The Boys in the Band* five years earlier. But while that film was a harrowing drama focused on questions of sexual identity and self-acceptance, here

> ❝ Here was an action thriller comedy with a gay antihero. Would audiences accept Sonny?

John Cazale (left) and Al Pacino (right) were old friends in real life, playing two wage-slave losers getting to know each other over the course of the robbery.

was an action thriller comedy with a gay antihero. Would audiences accept Sonny? Bregman explains the mindset behind the story's development: "[These guys] were normal human beings, with human emotions, in a bizarre setting. We didn't show them as freaks because we never considered them freaks." After reading Pierson's final script, Pacino reconsidered: here was role that was complex and sympathetic, volatile yet humane. And if he said no, Dustin Hoffman might snap it up.

The next key element was casting Sal Naturale (Pierson retained his first name in the script). The real Sal was just eighteen, an angry kid with a troubled past filled with juvenile detention centers and abuse. Since they'd be acting in lockstep with one another in nearly every scene, Lumet insisted that Pacino sit in on auditions; after dozens of maybes, Pacino suggested his friend John Cazale, with whom he'd just finished shooting Coppola's epic. The sleight, balding actor seemed all wrong for the role of the violent yet angelic Sal—until Cazale read for the part. Within two lines, Lumet was sold on Pacino's suggestion, and the two actors would craft a partnership on screen that was antithesis of what they'd just achieved in *The Godfather Part II*. Michael and Fredo

Sidney Lumet strove for realism whenever possible, opting for natural light and nixing a soundtrack score.

In August, 1972, Sonny Wortzik robbed a bank. 250 cops, the F.B.I., 8 hostages and 2,000 onlookers will never forget what took place.

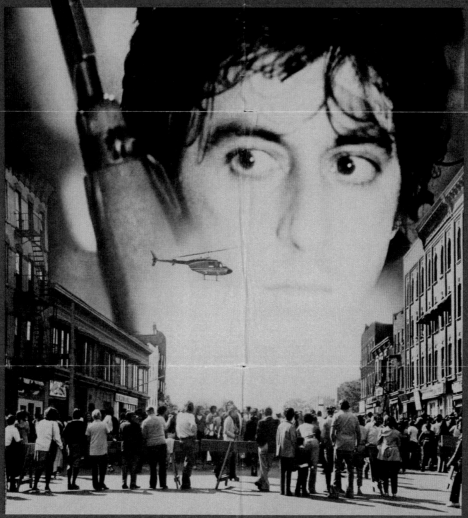

AL PACINO

An Artists Entertainment Complex Inc Production

DOG DAY AFTERNOON

Also Starring JOHN CAZALE · JAMES BRODERICK and CHARLES DURNING as Moretti
Screenplay by FRANK PIERSON · Produced by MARTIN BREGMAN and MARTIN ELFAND
Directed by SIDNEY LUMET · Film Editor DEDE ALLEN · TECHNICOLOR®
from WARNER BROS. A WARNER COMMUNICATIONS COMPANY

STYLE B

Pacino's Sonny Wortzik is a volatile live wire, who confronts instant fame and the prospect of losing everything over the course of one hot summer night.

Corleone are bonded by blood and weighed down with decades-long resentments and betrayals; in Lumet's film they are practically strangers, wage-slave losers betting double or nothing on an impossible dream.

The circus of August 22, 1972, was rivaled only by two months' shooting in Park Slope. Lumet insisted on three weeks of rehearsal before filming began, and rather than asking the supporting players cast as the bank workers to imitate the actual captives, the actors were encouraged to dress in their own clothes and stretch and rework Pierson's scripted lines to suit their own vernacular. This process forged a bond among the cast and aided their sense of familiarity on screen. Cinematographer Victor Kemper utilized natural or naturally present artificial lighting for every scene, to strip any element of stylization from the action; Lumet also eschewed a music score of any kind, explaining: "It was so important to me that an audience believe that it really happened because what happened was so outrageous." A general call for extras to fill out the crowd grew each successive evening, with up to 3,000 locals turning out every night to watch the show and become a part of it.

The film's mordant humor came from everywhere: reports from the hostages in Kluge and Moore's original article, Pierson's script, Lumet's extensive rehearsals, and in-the-moment improvisations. According to Kluge and Moore, bank manager Robert Barrett told Wojtowicz, "I'm supposed to hate you guys, but I've had more laughs tonight than I've had in weeks." Pacino's difficulty in opening a gift box in which his shotgun is concealed during the film's first moments was an on-screen accident that hints at other unintentionally funny moments to come. In a scene where Sonny tells Sal that the FBI are furnishing them with a jet to leave the United States, he asks his friend where he might like to go. Cazale gives a considerate pause before solemnly replying: "Wyoming," a line improvised by the actor. Lumet chose newcomer Chris Sarandon to play Leon,

the character based on Aron, and while Sarandon and Pacino never meet on camera their long, plaintive phone call to each other is heartrending and poignant, with lines derived from Pierson's interviews with Aron as well as Lumet's incisive note to Sarandon during his audition: "Less Blanche DuBois, more Queens housewife."

> "What happened then was either more or less than the robbers deserved." —Kluge and Moore, "The Boys in the Bank"

Lumet's concern about the audience's reaction to Sonny was unfounded. Thanks to the respectful treatment of his relationship with Leon, and the realistic foundation the film had achieved by

> " Up to 3,000 locals [turned] out every night to watch the show and become a part of it.

In the middle of a robbery--
Mama comes to help.

Mama comes to help??

In the middle of a robbery--
An obscene phone call.

An obscene phone call??

Weird things can happen on a
DOG DAY AFTERNOON

AL PACINO
in DOG DAY
AFTERNOON

An Artists Entertainment Complex Inc Production
Also starring JOHN CAZALE · JAMES BRODERICK and CHARLES DURNING as Moretti · Screenplay by FRANK PIERSON
Produced by MARTIN BREGMAN and MARTIN ELFAND · Directed by SIDNEY LUMET · Film Editor DEDE ALLEN · TECHNICOLOR®
From WARNER BROS. A WARNER COMMUNICATIONS COMPANY

enhancing the natural whenever possible, *Dog Day Afternoon* was a smash hit with audiences and critics. It touched on not only the underrepresented topic of gay life in the 1970s, but also the transformative glare of the media spotlight that conflated infamy with fame in the pursuit of ratings. (Lumet's next film, *Network* [1976], built on that theme to a crescendo of satire and terror.) The film was nominated for six Academy Awards for Best Picture, Best Director, Best Actor, Best Original Screenplay, Best Supporting Actor, and Best Editing, and Pierson won for his script (the film had the misfortune of competing against *One Flew over the Cuckoo's Nest* [1975], which swept the ceremony).

A breakthrough role in the portrayal of a gay man in mainstream film belied a more complex reality. Many in the gay community, particularly those in GAA, saw Wojtowicz's criminal behavior and theatrics as a severe hindrance to their cause. They did not want this macho, foul-mouthed live wire representing them and their movement. When Wojtowicz returned to the Brooklyn branch of Chase Manhattan in the late 1970s with a news crew to sign autographs and pose for photos in a shirt that said "I ROBBED THIS BANK," teller and former hostage Santa Strazella bitterly remarked: "[He's] signing autographs and becoming a big star—making money on an ordeal he put a lot of people through."

While Wojtowicz failed to achieve his original goal in the robbery, he succeeded in selling that failure to Hollywood. While the total amount he received from the Warner Bros. was determined privately after decades of litigation, he used the initial $7,500 advance sent to him in 1975 to pay for Aron's gender reassignment surgery. Aron changed her name to Liz Eden, cut all ties with her husband, and eventually moved to upstate New York. In prison, Wojtowicz's status as a celebrity criminal saved him from abuse in some cases and fostered it in others—Pierson's invented subplot that Sonny may or may not have been complicit with the FBI in serving up Sal to their gunfire branded the real-life robber a rat. After the film was shown at Lewisburg Prison, Wojtowicz was attacked several times. Through a series of legal maneuvers he got his sentence reduced; when he was released in April 1978 he tried to make up for his unemployable status as an ex-con by cashing in on his enduring fame, nicknaming himself "The Dog" and explaining to anyone within earshot his pivotal relationship to the film. Wojtowicz even applied to work as a security guard at Chase Manhattan, explaining to them that "Nobody's gonna rob The Dog's bank."

After the success of *Dog Day Afternoon*, Pacino's winning streak ended with *Bobby Deerfield* (1977), a languid romance about a race car driver's doomed affair with a fatally ill socialite that tanked at the box office. In *Cruising* (1980), his portrayal of a naive cop who goes undercover in lower Manhattan's S&M gay subculture pushed the envelope further than the role of Sonny, but the film's uneven plot, protests during the film's production by gay activist groups, and Pacino's clashes with director William Friedkin branded the film as notorious rather than entertaining and it became hard to find in subsequent decades. Over the next twenty years Pacino went on to finally net an Oscar (for *Scent of a Woman* [1992]) and achieve cult-film immortality as Tony Montana in Brian De Palma's *Scarface* (1983), but his credits since 1975 inspired him to remark to biographer Lawrence Grobel in 2009: "I haven't made a good film since *Dog Day Afternoon*."

As for the real bank employees, they returned to work and went on with their lives, never forgetting August 1972. Josephine Tutino, a teller haunted by the ordeal, worked through her trauma by writing the song "Lollipops & Shotguns (A Hostage's Lament)," which her husband had privately recorded. The resulting pop song transcends novelty and is a bona fide swinger, with backup singers and the catchy (if macabre) hook, "Eating lollipops with shotguns aimed at your eyes / Eating lollipops with danger at your side." As Tutino recalled years later, "I had to write it down just to get it out of me."

In the ensuing decades, Wojtowicz's memory of his actions that night became blended with Pacino's portrayal.

"I'm the bank robber, fuck Al Pacino."
—John Wojtowicz

In the twenty-first century a new generation of filmmakers, raised on *Dog Day Afternoon*, approached Wojtowicz and asked him for his story. Wojtowicz was as mercurial and difficult as ever, demanding that callers ask to speak with The Dog, not John, and railing about Warner Bros.'s continued reluctance to pay him his full share of the film's profits. French media artist Pierre Huyghe endured Wojtowicz's eccentricities to create *The Third Memory* (2000), a short film in which Wojtowicz returns to a studio-build replica of the bank (tellingly it's the film's fictional First Brooklyn Savings Bank, not the real Chase Manhattan branch) and directs the action and narrates what everyone did and said on that fateful day. The resulting ten-minute film displays how much Wojtowicz's memory of the events is infected with scenes from Lumet's film, and every aspect of that day's action in his mind's eye paints him as a romantic hero deeply wronged (he argues, contrary to other eyewitnesses' accounts, that Sal was murdered by FBI agents in cold blood after he had been disarmed, yet shows no remorse at the pivotal role he played in his friend's untimely death). Huyghe explained: "[My film] is not the memory of the event. John has no memory of the event, to be honest. And it's not the memory that he's built from all the media. It's what he creates, he takes a part of each thing and makes his own, new memory."

In the Dutch documentary *Based on a True Story* (2004), Richard Wandel, former president of GAA, puts it more succinctly: "I'm sure John to this day thinks of himself as quite a hero. But I think he's just foolish. . . . He still hasn't figured out what it's all about." Director Walter Stokman's film, like Pierson's mosaic of Wojtowicz, interviews many of the people involved with the incident besides The Dog, whose serpentine mind games with the filmmaker and demands for high sums over the phone are laced over contradictory impressions of that day from tellers, FBI agent James Murphy, and archival footage of Liz Eden. (Eden was not interviewed for the film, as she succumbed to AIDS in 1987.) Wojtowicz was finally interviewed at length in *The Dog* (2013), a thorough portrait of the man's life by Allison Berg and Frank Keraudren that displays his bravado, charm, and fuzzy relationship to the truth; it also depicts his fight with cancer, a struggle that claimed Wojtowicz in 2009. Wojtowicz's children did not participate in either documentary; his ex-wife Carmen explains that their son, Sean, wants nothing to do with his father. But, Sean's favorite movie star? Al Pacino.

"You gotta get fun out of life."
—Sonny Wortzik

Dog Day Afternoon's themes of alienation, LGBTQ+ life, gender identity, and media madness read like a treatment for a script currently in production rather than a film approaching its fiftieth birthday. Despite its heavy topics, its success lies in the fact that the story is anything but—it's also an entertaining heist film about love, community, and acceptance. Pacino's Sonny Wortzik may not have been an exact duplication of John Wojtowicz, but who was Wojtowicz exactly during those moments in the bank, with Pacino's line "I'll make him an offer he can't refuse" still ringing in his head? The pieces will never match up, but the myriad realities of August 22, 1972, continue to loop in a möbius strip that is endlessly compelling. ∎

Born to Lose is being expanded to a book, forthcoming from Headpress in 2025.

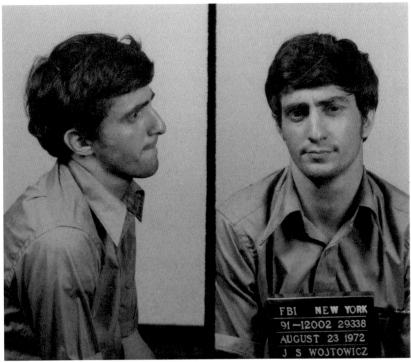
Wojtowicz's mugshot, the day one reality ended for him and a new one began.

NOIR CITY

e-Magazine

Back Issues

BURDEN OF PROOF

COLD CASE NOIR

By Danilo Castro

Hollywood has always been at odds with the truth. Studios love capitalizing on the public's interest in real-life stories by adapting them for the big screen, but as we all know, real life is too complicated to fit a three-act structure. Concessions are made, whether it be in the form of an imagined character or a shuffling of historical events to reach a more dramatic conclusion. As long as the reshaped story bears a resemblance to what actually happened, and the fictionalized elements are entertaining, studios assume that audiences will be satisfied.

Satisfaction becomes elusive, however, when the real-life story has no conclusion. There have been numerous attempts to make films about unsolved crimes, but the thing that makes these cases appealing in theory is the very thing that makes them difficult to adapt. They invalidate the three-act structure. They provide a tantalizing premise without any of the payoff. These films—let's call them "cold case adaptations"—have been especially prevalent in the twenty-first century, and what makes them worthy of discussion is that each takes a different approach to the same narrative challenge. They use the negative space afforded them to develop an even more ambiguous style of noir.

The murder of Elizabeth Short inspired other books and films besides Ellroy's *The Black Dahlia*. *True Confessions* (1981, above) recreated the infamous crime scene, as did the 1975 TV movie *Who Is the Black Dahlia?* (directed by noir veteran Joe Pevney), in which Lucy Arnaz played the ill-fated Short.

Of these cold case adaptations, *The Black Dahlia* (2006) has the most complicated relationship with the truth. The film is based on the James Ellroy novel of the same name, which in turn is based on the grisly murder of Elizabeth Short. The well-known details, including the discovery of Short's body in a vacant lot and the media circus that ensued, are accurately portrayed. The investigation that follows, however, takes a lot of creative liberties, most notably finding a culprit for that infamous crime in January 1947.

The real Elizabeth Short waited tables and lived off of Hollywood Boulevard. The fictional Short (Mia Kirshner) is at the fulcrum of Hollywood decadence, making stag films and fraternizing with old money when she isn't performing humiliating screen tests. *The Black Dahlia* makes no bones about which version is more scintillating, both for the viewer and the fictional detectives assigned to the case. Dwight "Bucky" Bleichert (Josh Hartnett) and Lee Blanchard (Aaron Eckhart) become so obsessed with Short that perverse side effects take root in their personal lives. The former romances a Short lookalike, while the latter turns abusive toward his longtime girlfriend.

Blurring the lines between fact and fiction is not inherently a bad thing. Ellroy's novel is a brilliant mashup of pulp and tabloid myths, and the film follows suit. At least, it tries to. The original cut ran three hours, with screen time dedicated to real-life figures like Marjorie Graham and Robert "Red" Manley, as well as the psychological toll the case takes on Bleichert over several years. Universal Pictures demanded it be whittled down to 120 minutes, which meant condensing the plot and scrapping the aforementioned characters. The studio also emphasized the tagline "inspired by true events" during the film's promotion. Director Brian de Palma took issue with both of these decisions. In his estimation, they created a disconnect between what film audiences got and what they *thought* they were getting.

The film's scandalized depiction of Elizabeth Short (above) has little in common with the real woman (below).

I'm not here to reclaim *The Black Dahlia* as some lost masterpiece. It's a mess, and it's hard to imagine a longer runtime would have smoothed over the terrible lead performances and stilted presentation. I will point to the climax, however, as an example of something the film gets right. Bleichert forces a confession out of deranged socialite Ramona Linscott (Fiona Shaw), but she shoots herself before he can make the arrest. The detective can't prove a thing, and the Short case remains officially unsolved. It's a seminal noir wrinkle, and a clever way of rewriting history while maintaining the same, bleak outcome.

Hollywoodland (2006) is about a person trying to rewrite history in real time. Louis Simo (Adrien Brody) is a private detective who's more than willing to fabricate a headline if it means a few more bucks in his pocket. He looks into the death of *Adventures of Superman* star George Reeves (Ben Affleck) despite it being ruled a suicide, and the first thing he does is sidle up to the press and spread rumors of foul play. It's 1959, still the golden age of celebrity gossip. The kicker, of course, is that the more Simo digs up about the actor, the more the detective comes to believe his own press.

Simo is based on celebrity gumshoe–author Milo Speriglio, and the decision to tell the story from his perspective gives *Hollywood-*

> ## It's a seminal noir wrinkle, and a clever way of rewriting history while maintaining the same, bleak outcome.

land a basis in reality. The operative word here being *basis*. Simo doesn't have a shred of evidence, but his tenacity, coupled with the bizarre circumstances in which Reeves's body was found, make for an admittedly persuasive argument. Why were there no fingerprints on the actor's gun? Why were there bullet holes in the floor of his bedroom? The police officers handling the case fail to provide satisfying answers, much like their real-life counterparts. They'd rather maintain the status quo than rock the boat of powerful studio executives like Eddie Mannix (Bob Hoskins).

Simo hits the same roadblocks. His investigation leads to skirmishes with Reeves's fiancée, Leonore Lemmon (Robin Tunney), and his former mistress, Toni Mannix (Diane Lane), now married to the aforementioned exec. Their fraught relationships with the actor are shown through increasingly dismal flashbacks. The film is at its best during these passages, carefully building motives for each of the characters while presenting Reeves as an imperfect charmer. He was a superhero who couldn't seem to figure out life as a regular

Ben Affleck was cast as George Reeves after scheduling conflicts forced the studio's original choice, Hugh Jackman, to drop out.

Fiancee Had Premonition
Television's 'Superman' Ends Life With Pistol
Actor George Reeves Had Argued With Guests

HOLLYWOOD, June 16 (UPI) — Actor George Reeves, TV's "Superman," fatally shot himself in the head early today with a German Luger pistol in a suicide which police said was predicted by the "woman's intuition" of his fiancee.

Police found the body of the 45-year-old actor sprawled on the blood-splattered bed of his Benedict Canyon home in Beverly Hills.

The bullet entered the right side of the husky actor's head, emerged through his left temple and imbedded itself in a wall.

Detective Don Johnson said Reeves had gone to bed about midnight and the actor's house guests, fiancee Leonore Lemmon, 35, of New York City, and Robert Condon, a writer, also from New York, were preparing to retire when some friends came by for a visit.

Mr. Johnson said Reeves came down to the living room from his upstairs bedroom and objected to the late hour visit of William Bliss of Hollywood and Miss Carol Von Ronkel, who also lives in the canyon.

"He was irritated about the friends arriving, and he ordered them out," Mr. Johnson said. "But then the argument was settled and Reeves went back to his room.

"When he went back to

GEORGE REEVES
Luger at his side.

Reeves Booked Here July 4

LENORE LEMMON
Fiancee of Reeves.

Simo (Adrien Brody, right) may be based on Milo Speriglio, but the character is significantly older, and his troubled personal life is invented for the film.

The production had trees flown in via helicopter to make sure the Lake Berryessa murder site looked exactly like it did in 1969.

guy. Simo winds up having the opposite problem. He gets a chance to patch things up with his estranged son (a Superman fan, naturally), but he doesn't get to break open the case in heroic fashion. He still believes it's foul play, he just can't figure out what kind.

The film can't, either. Instead of extrapolating a conclusion, *Hollywoodland* goes the multiple-choice route, presenting three different versions of Reeves's death: accidental shooting by Lemmon, murder by one of Mannix's goons, and suicide. These scenarios are well-staged by director Allen Coulter, and each is given the necessary context to be convincing. The decision to end with the actor's suicide, however, gives the film an unexpected poignancy. Reeves was so closely tied to the role of Superman it became his albatross. Having failed to get a production company off the ground, he was faced with having to put the tights back on shortly before his death. He was forty-five years old. It's telling that after two hours of proposed coverups, the simplest possibility is still the most tragic.

A decade after Reeves's death and a few hundred miles away, the Zodiac Killer began his reign of terror. The Zodiac transfixed the San Francisco Bay Area between 1968 and 1974, killing five people and taunting local newspapers with ciphers that supposedly revealed his identity. He threatened to shoot out the tires of school buses and the students on them unless his ciphers were published. David Fincher was one of these students. The future director was tailed by squad cars and told of the Zodiac's high-powered rifle by his dad, which may have sparked his career-long fascination with serial killers. Fincher briefly considered directing *The Black Dahlia*, but *Zodiac* (2007) gave him the rare opportunity to meld personal experience with formal precision, and the result was a genre-defining masterpiece.

The film's adherence to fact is exemplary. Fincher and screenwriter James Vanderbilt spent eighteen months researching the case to make sure that every crucial detail was accounted for. The only crimes depicted are the ones with surviving witnesses, and a different actor plays the Zodiac each time, to better illustrate the discrepancies that existed in the police descriptions. The friendship between *San Francisco Chronicle* cartoonist Robert Graysmith (Jake Gyllenhaal) and reporter Paul Avery (Robert Downey Jr.) is the biggest creative liberty taken, as the two men rarely crossed paths in their

Arthur Leigh Allen (John Carroll Lynch, above) is the closest *Zodiac* gets to a culprit. Despite his reputation for multiple takes, David Fincher (below) brought the film in under budget.

Brad Pitt and Daniel Craig were considered for the role of Paul Avery before Robert Downey Jr. (left) was cast. Jake Gyllenhaal (right) was the first choice for Robert Graysmith.

professional life. Their scenes are so important to the film's conceit, however, that I'm inclined to give it a pass. Graysmith and Avery bond over the case and are subsequently broken by it, with the former descending into obsession and the latter drinking himself into oblivion.

Graysmith's compulsiveness is introduced as a boyish quirk. He's late submitting a cartoon because he tries to solve one of the Zodiac's ciphers. Avery mocks him, and SFPD inspector Dave Toschi (Mark Ruffalo) barely knows who he is. He even manages to charm his future wife, Melanie (Chloë Sevigny), by turning their first date into part of the investigation. The second half of Zodiac probes Graysmith's dark side. As more time passes and the police involved with the case either retire or get reassigned, the more fanatically determined Graysmith becomes. He wakes up Toschi in the middle of the night with new leads and pursues suspects that were dismissed years earlier. Threatening phone calls do little to deter him from writing his own book about the case (upon which the film is based). Zodiac threads the needle between subjectivity and objectivity; the viewer is compelled enough to share Graysmith's curiosity but removed enough to fear the consequences of his actions.

Graysmith tracks down his prime suspect, Arthur Leigh Allen (John Carroll Lynch), in the film's penultimate scene. He looks Allen in the eye, lingers for a moment, and then walks away. No arrest, no confession, no catharsis. Zodiac doesn't know who its titular killer is, and it defies other cold case adaptations by turning this ambiguity into a dramatic strength. The tension doesn't come from a clever

twist, but from wondering how many years of their lives Graysmith and Toschi will sacrifice before finally calling it a day. "Do you know more people die in the East Bay commute every three months than that idiot ever killed?" The question, posed by Avery, sums up the futility of the whole affair. Fincher may have modeled his film on *All the President's Men* (1976), but in depicting the failed efforts of real-life people, Zodiac assumes a worldview far more nihilistic—and far more noir—than its predecessor.

> " *Zodiac* doesn't know who its titular killer is, and it defies other cold case adaptations by turning this ambiguity into a dramatic strength.

Detectives Park (Song Kang-ho, left) and Seo (Kim Sang-kyung, right). Kim slept fewer hours during production to give his character a haggard appearance.

Memories of Murder (2003) was linked to *Zodiac* before either film existed. The former is based on the Hwaseong serial murders that occurred between 1986 and 1991, and the culprit behind them was referred to as the "Korean Zodiac Killer." Bong Joon-ho was intrigued by the country's decision to ape Western iconography, and the writer-director explores this uneasy dynamic throughout the film. Characters are constantly referencing US shows and parroting English phrases. In one crucial instance, the police are forced to send evidence to the United States because they don't have the technology to process it themselves. *Memories of Murder* takes on the same cold case themes as its peers, but the decision to frame them as symptoms of a stifled, autocratic government provides a rich subtext.

The Hwaseong police are doomed from the start, and their inexperience can be gleaned from the differing methods of their detectives. Park Doo-man (Song Kang-ho) vows to find the killer

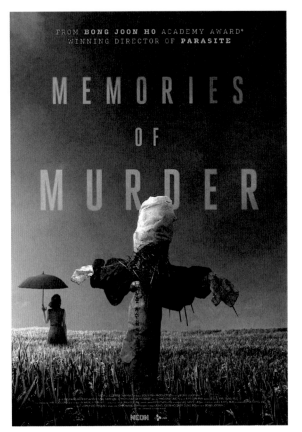

through intuition. He prides himself on being able to tell if a man is guilty by simply looking him in the eye. Seo Tae-yoon (Kim Sang-kyung) values facts, and is quick to rule out a suspect if he doesn't check all the boxes. The film charts the slow, agonizing realization that neither method is working. Park's instincts lead to the wrong man being charged, and when he runs out of easy targets, he resorts to magic potions to summon the killer. Seo has promising theories, but his discipline breaks down when he tries to shoot a suspect whose DNA results are inconclusive. Park stops him, signifying a breaking point of his own. He is forced to consider, for the first time, whether any of it matters.

The epilogue is a chilling embodiment of the film's title. It's 2003 and Park has changed careers. An impromptu visit to the first crime scene leads to him being told that another man recently made the same pilgrimage. The man was apparently reminiscing on something he did long ago, and upon hearing this, Park reverts to his old self. He turns toward the camera and stares, desperate for more information. The film has none to offer, however. Fade to black. Once more, a director finds a novel way to address the unresolved. Breaking the fourth wall allows Bong to pass the burden of proof onto the viewer, so we must continue to ask questions after the credits roll. Unless, of course, the viewer has something to hide. Bong was certain the actual Korean Zodiac Killer would see *Memories of Murder*, and he wanted an ending that would make him feel seen in return. The killer was going to look Park in the eye, whether he liked it or not.

Bong was right. Lee Choon-jae confessed to the Hwaseong serial murders in 2019, after his DNA was linked to one of the victims. He could not be prosecuted for the murders due to the statute of limitations, but he was already serving a life sentence for killing his sister-in-law in 1994. Lee was given the chance to watch *Memories of Murder* during a 2020 court case, and while his response was predictably sociopathic ("I had no feelings or emotions toward the movie"), there's a satisfaction in knowing that the director reached his intended target. Justice was belatedly served. *Memories of Murder* is the rare cold case adaptation that's been solved after the fact, but it has not been diminished as a result. If anything, the film's predictive storytelling has allowed it to play better now than when it was originally released.

The Black Dahlia, *Hollywoodland*, *Zodiac*, and *Memories of Murder* were released in the span of five years, and their respective approaches can be summarized as: fiction, speculation, dramatization, and manifestation. They were by no means the first, but in surveying the last decade of cold case films, the quartet proves useful as a template. *The Irishman* (2019) spun a fictional narrative around the disappearance of Jimmy Hoffa, and despite receiving criticism from Hoffa scholars, the film earned ten Oscar nominations. *Boston Strangler* (2023) was a blatant *Zodiac* homage, right down to the period setting and the protagonist being a journalist, while *The Night of the 12th* (2022) won six César Awards for its Bongian depiction of an unsolved murder.

In the original film noir era, endings were mostly decisive. The killer is put behind bars, the crook botches the heist, the femme fatale gets blown away. The cold case noir takes it a step further by proposing the only thing worse than tragedy: uncertainty. We're wired as moviegoers to make sense of the mysteries laid out before us, so when the opportunity to do so is removed, our deepest anxieties fill the void and our desire to learn the truth grows tenfold. The films discussed here reconcile these contradictory feelings, and in doing so, they say more about the human condition than a proper conclusion ever could. ∎

STRANGER THAN FICTION

Cold cases are more popular than ever. You'd be hard-pressed to find an unsolved murder that hasn't been extensively covered by a podcast or a documentary miniseries. That being said, no coverage has been as bizarre or as revelatory as that of Robert Durst. The son of a New York real estate magnate, Durst was a suspect in three different crimes: the disappearance of his wife, Kathleen McCormack, in 1982, the murder of his friend Susan Berman in 2000, and the death of his neighbor Morris Black in 2001.

All Good Things (2010) dramatizes these crimes, and the conspicuous ways in which Durst avoided punishment. The film changes the names of those involved—including Durst, who becomes David Marks (Ryan Gosling)—but the rest of the story is based on case files and interviews director Andrew Jarecki conducted with Durst's associates. *All Good Things* is an engaging thriller, its most notable attribute being its refusal to give a definitive take on what happened. This tact was noted by Durst of all people, who sang Jarecki's praises and even recorded a commentary with the director for the film's DVD release.

Durst's comfort with Jarecki, a documentarian by trade, was unprecedented. The millionaire had never discussed his personal life, and yet he agreed to star in the documentary miniseries *The Jinx: The Life and Deaths of Robert Durst* (2015) as a means of dispelling his lurid reputation. Instead, the miniseries confirmed it. Durst's interviews with Jarecki, which were conducted over several years, present a disquieting and unreliable figure. He admits to fabricating an alibi the night his wife disappeared, and he's shockingly cavalier about the fact that he was accused of murdering Black while pretending to be a mute woman named Dorothy Ciner.

The Jinx moves through its six episodes with verve. The nonlinear structure and the flashy opening credits make it clear that the show aims to entertain, but never at the expense of its serious subject matter. In the finale, Jarecki confronts Durst with newly discovered evidence, and the millionaire is visibly flummoxed. Durst excuses himself to use the restroom and, forgetting his microphone is still on, mumbles the words: "What the hell did I do? Killed them all, of course." It's a jaw-dropping moment, a genuine instance of reality proving stranger than fiction. Durst tried to walk back his comment afterward, but the damage had been done. He was charged with Berman's murder and arrested the day before the episode aired. He was sentenced to life in prison in 2021, where he would die the following year.

Durst prompting his own downfall is dramatic irony at its finest, but even more incredible is the fact that Jarecki leveraged a film without a resolution into a miniseries that provided one. He recontextualized his own cold case adaptation by solving the case. It's such a singular achievement that any survey of true crime in which the director isn't mentioned is incomplete.

—Danilo Castro

10 RILLINGTON PLACE

THE STORY OF THE
CHRISTIE
SEX-MURDERS!

COLUMBIA PICTURES Presents

RICHARD ATTENBOROUGH · JUDY GEESON · JOHN HURT

MARTIN RANSOHOFF-LESLIE LINDER "10 RILLINGTON PLACE"x
PRODUCTION

Screenplay by CLIVE EXTON · Associate Producer BASIL APPLEBY · Produced by LESLIE LINDER and MARTIN RANSOHOFF · Directed by RICHARD FLEISCHER · COLOUR

Richard Fleischer may not be the first name that comes to mind when listing film noir's greatest directors, but his noir credentials are impressive. After directing two successful B pictures at RKO, the amnesia noir *The Clay Pigeon* (1949) and *Bodyguard* (1948), Fleischer moved to Eagle-Lion for *Trapped* (1949) before returning to RKO for *Follow Me Quietly* (1949). The director cited this film as a turning point, stating, "This is the film that, above all, increased my knowledge of the trade. I learned how to organize a film."

Fleischer took advantage of the knowledge and skills he learned during *Follow Me Quietly* to direct other notable noir titles *Armored Car Robbery* (1950), *His Kind of Woman* (1951, uncredited), *The*

Narrow Margin (1952), and *Violent Saturday* (1955), as well as true crime pictures with strong noir elements: *Compulsion* (1959), a fictionalized account of the 1924 Leopold and Loeb murder trial, and *The Boston Strangler* (1968), loosely based on the story of serial killer Albert DeSalvo. Yet the director once told Eddie Muller that *10 Rillington Place* (1971), the story of British serial killer John Christie, was the "most noir film" he'd ever made.

10 Rillington Place not only retains the actual names of the principal players, but also used dialogue taken from documented sources and was filmed in the London location where the murders took place. Yet the film's relevance far surpasses most stories "based on actual events." Adapted from

the book *Ten Rillington Place* (1961) by Ludovic Kennedy, Clive Exton's screenplay walks a fine line between true crime and horror, adding an examination of two topics of ongoing debate: abortion and capital punishment.

John Christie (Richard Attenborough) is simultaneously the film's most fascinating and disturbing character. In the story's opening, set in 1944, Christie lures a local acquaintance named Muriel (Phyllis MacMahon) into his Notting Hill flat, assuring the woman that he can cure her bronchitis with a method apparently dismissed by most doctors. Donning owllike glasses and speaking mostly in calm whispers with a slight lisp, Christie presents himself as an intelligent yet reserved middle-aged man

British serial killer John Christie (left) is portrayed by Richard Attenborough in one of his finest, most disturbing performances.

seeking only to help Muriel. Had this scene taken place in an actual medical facility, we might trust Christie completely. The unshakable confidence he displays with his patient invites a certain level of assurance. Yet the audience suspects what Muriel does not, that the gas delivered by a rubber tube is meant to debilitate rather than relax the young woman. Too late, Muriel comes to the realization that Christie's intent is not to help her but to end her life for his own twisted sexual gratification.

Jumping to 1949, Christie and his wife, Ethel (Pat Heywood), rent out their property's upper-story flat to a young family: Timothy (John Hurt) and Beryl Evans (Judy Geeson) and their infant daughter. Timothy seems reluctant to accept this squalid dwelling in such an uninviting neighborhood, yet Christie's quietly manipulative method of influencing the Evanses, informing them there's another couple "very keen" on the place, rush them into accepting. Learning that Timothy can neither read nor write ignites opportunities for further machinations in Christie's mind. Although five years have passed in the narrative, the film's opening scene remains fresh in the viewer's mind, spurring fears about what crimes Christie may unleash on the unsuspecting Evans family.

Christie and Evans are both liars, but miles apart in their degrees of deception. At a local pub Timothy boasts of his job and sexual prowess, yet the regulars can see right through him, knowing that his stories are nothing more than wishful fantasies. Timothy is forced to step up his lying game after Christie promises Beryl that he can perform her abortion (illegal at the time in the UK), but instead kills and sexually assaults her. Yet Christie is a master liar and manipulator, explaining to Timothy that Beryl's abortion was not only unsuccessful but also the cause of her death. Christie's fabricated lament—"If she had only come to me sooner"—both excuses himself and places the blame on Evans. Christie uses Timothy's anger and confusion to further spin the situation in a way that makes the husband complicit. "So who are the police going to believe?" Christie taunts, "You? Or me, that was a special constable for four years?" The killer then instructs Timothy to stay with his aunt and uncle near Cardiff, telling him to make up some story to appease them. Now, with much more at stake than deceiving a few mates at the pub, Timothy realizes how difficult it is to lie when you're not very good at it.

Christie also understands that Timothy's impulsive nature will help falsely implicate him. Earlier scenes of the couple arguing give evidence of Timothy's rage and lack of control as he shouts and breaks objects in the flat. These episodes are also loud enough to be overheard by neighbors, supporting Christie's later testimony that Timothy is a violent man who could easily have strangled Beryl in a fit of anger. Christie may portray himself as a calm, middle-aged gentleman, but he is instead a cold, calculating manipulator who will do anything to help shift the blame from himself to Timothy.

With fabricated evidence and twisted statements coming primarily from Christie, Timothy's murder trial proves to be a juggernaut that totally overwhelms the helpless young man. While Christie's victims had little time to react to the truth of what was happening to them, Evans is given the opportunity to defend himself but lacks the capacity to do so.

In no time at all Evans is convicted and sentenced to be executed for the murder of his wife and young daughter (whom Christie also killed). As much as the audience is filled with escalating turmoil at this injustice, the greatest injustice of all occurs as Evans is swiftly taken to a small room, hooded, noosed, and hanged in a matter of seconds. Perhaps even more chilling is the fact that the film's technical advisor, Albert Pierrepoint, was actually the man who executed Evans. Years later, after Christie was convicted of killing Beryl, Evans's wrongful execution was one of the primary reasons why capital punishment was abolished in the UK in 1965, and it still stands as a sobering moment for contemporary audiences.

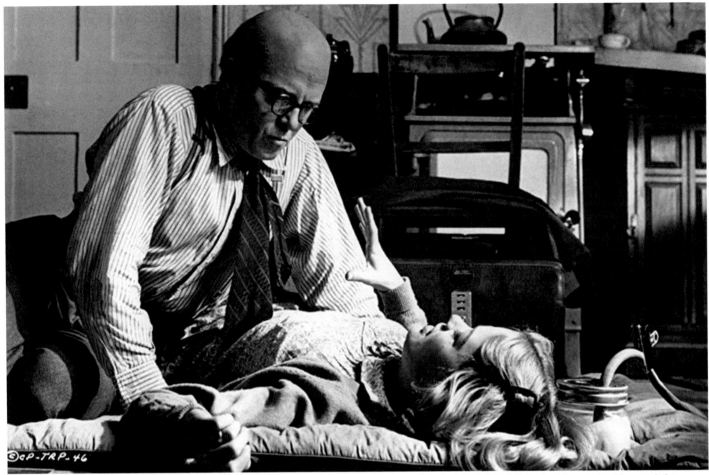

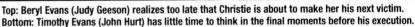
Top: Beryl Evans (Judy Geeson) realizes too late that Christie is about to make her his next victim.
Bottom: Timothy Evans (John Hurt) has little time to think in the final moments before his execution.

Fleischer's previous true crime pictures were all based on twentieth-century cases in the United States, but *10 Rillington Place* forgoes not only American settings, but also more lurid subjects from Britain's own history as represented in such earlier works as David Lean's *Madeleine* (1950), John Gilling's *The Flesh and the Fiends* (1960), and a whole host of Jack the Ripper movies, all of which are set in the nineteenth century. This film draws much of its disturbing atmosphere from a backdrop of fear and desperation resulting from World War II. The fact that the site of the murders was still standing as Fleischer was filming gives harsh evidence that this atrocity was true, and its presence provided a warning that its horror was still evident. (The site of the murders was demolished soon after the film was completed, removing any physical reminders of the tragedies that took place there.)

The almost complete absence of a musical score heightens the hor-ror and tragedy of the murders, not only as the victims' confidence and trust in Christie are ripped away, but also as the intimacy of their final experiences continues to haunt us: Christie's craggy breathing resonating in our ears, his alarming black eyes inches from our own, and the dismal surroundings closing in on us.

10 Rillington Place contains no hint of the sensationalism frequently found in true crime films. Its faithfulness to the events, the documented words spoken, and the location makes the film far more chilling than most of the stories we see based on actual incidents. When the film is over, we feel that we have stood in the same flat where Muriel and Beryl were violated and murdered. We hear Christie's whispers, and we—like Timothy Evans—stand watching the preparations for an execution that we are powerless to prevent. In all these ways and more, Fleischer puts the "true" back in true crime through an unwavering commitment to authenticity, delivering one of cinema's most disturbing and horrific films based on actual events. ∎

NOIR OR NOT
Steve Kronenberg

Tim O'Kelly's Bobby Thompson puts one of his many *Targets* in the crosshairs of his rifle.

TARGETS

Targets (1968) is as important as it is underrated. It was writer-director Peter Bogdanovich's first feature film, and while it's generally viewed as an anti-gun polemic, its tone, theme, and style mark it as a genuine neo-noir. Taking a cue from *Sunset Boulevard* (1950), Bogdanovich infused his screenplay with a "meta" mindset, casting Boris Karloff as an elderly horror film veteran on the verge of retirement. *Targets* also takes noir into uncharted territory, cleverly conflating the end of Hollywood's golden age with the cynicism and dissolution that would begin to plague the United States in the late 1960s.

Playing a mirror image of himself, Karloff is Byron Orlok, an aging bogeyman who feels irrelevant and outdated. Bogdanovich

cast himself as Sammy Michaels, the director of Orlok's last film, *The Terror* (which is in fact a slapdash 1963 production Karloff made for B-movie icon Roger Corman). While meeting with Michaels to discuss his impending retirement, Orlok scans a newspaper headline about a mass murder and realizes that the harmless cinematic horrors of the 1930s pale in comparison to the atrocities occurring in contemporary America. "My kind of horror isn't horror anymore," he laments. At Michaels's urging, Orlok reluctantly agrees to a final personal appearance at a screening of *The Terror*, to be held at Los Angeles's Reseda Drive-In. He's also in the crosshairs of a rifle held by a young man named Bobby Thompson (Tim O'Kelly), who's testing his aim while pur-

chasing the piece from a gun shop located across the street from Michaels's office. "I always wanted a rifle like this," he tells the shopkeeper, before adding it to an arsenal stored in the trunk of his car. Thompson's boyish persona and squeaky-clean garb mask a disturbed soul. Living a dull, placid life in an LA suburb, he seethes with frustration. "I don't know what's happening to me," he tells his wife (Tanya Morgan). "I get funny ideas." Suddenly and without provocation or motive, he robotically guns down his wife, his mother, and a teen delivering groceries before embarking on a shooting spree that takes him from the San Diego Freeway to the Reseda Drive-In and a climactic confrontation with Orlok.

Though shot in late 1967, *Targets* wasn't

Left: A deceptively affable photo of mass murderer Charles Whitman on whom *Targets* was based. Right: Thompson confronts his doomed wife in this eerie scene from *Targets*.

released until August 1968, mere months after the assassinations of Martin Luther King Jr. and Robert Kennedy. The film bears a sensibility both wistful and frightening, augmented by fine performances from Karloff and O'Kelly. Disabled and frail, the eighty-year-old Karloff effectively captures Orlok's disillusion, coupling avuncular amiability with bitterness and heartbreak. His interplay with Bogdanovich and Nancy Hsueh, who plays his assistant, is especially poignant. Karloff's sad eyes were always those of a monster with a soul. (His beautifully rendered one-take recitation of the Arabian fable "Appointment in Samarra" drew a standing ovation from the film's cast and crew.) Bogdanovich's script touched Karloff deeply, and he agreed to offer additional days of service for free. He lived just long enough to enjoy lavish praise for his performance before his death on February 2, 1969, at age eighty-one.

Karloff embodies the film's elegiac tone, but it's O'Kelly's laconic loner who gives *Targets* its unnerving edge. Thompson is an amalgam of the mediocre and the monstrous. His performance is free of pretense and artifice, stripped down to underplayed, faceless psychopathy. We cringe as we see him sipping a soda while coolly picking off motorists on the San Diego Freeway and families at the Reseda Drive-In. Thompson's well-scrubbed looks and obsession

with guns may remind noir fans of Bart Tare in *Gun Crazy* (1950), but Thompson lacks Tare's vulnerability. He's more a taciturn Norman Bates.

Targets owes much of its noir acidity to Bogdanovich's somber style and László Kovács's gritty cinematography. Kovács's camera trails Thompson through Los Angeles's grimiest neighborhoods, grimly depicting a flat, soulless landscape that mirrors the gunman's own emotional void. When

Thompson murders his family, Kovács comes in tight and close, using POV shots to emphasize the scene's random brutality. He weaponizes the zoom lens, using it to capture each of Thompson's victims through the crosshairs of a rifle just before the trigger is pulled. Bogdanovich's then-wife, Polly Platt, who also cowrote the picture, assisted Kovács in devising appropriate lighting for both lead characters: Orlok is surrounded by warm, white hues, while Thompson's non-

Boris Karloff and Peter Bogdanovich discuss horrors past and present in this candid shot taken during filming.

descript killer is bathed in bland blues and impenetrable darkness, a ghostly silhouette skulking through his suburban home. (Platt cited the simplicity of Don Siegel's noirs as a primary stylistic influence.) Kovács's visual imagination turns the film's final scene into a hallucinatory nightmare. We see Thompson's drive-in massacre through his eyes, as we watch the real Orlok advancing toward him while the celluloid Orlok stalks the sets of *The Terror* on the theater's enormous screen.

Unlike *The Sniper* (1952), another noir about a serial shooter, *Targets* is not focused on police procedure or psychological profiling. We know little about Bobby Thompson and even less about his pathology. Bogdanovich's approach is cold and detached, suffused with an unsettling quietude. The only concession to a soundtrack is the occasional source music emanating from the radio in Thompson's car. Family gatherings at his home are deceptively reserved and restrained. Credit Bogdanovich, Kovács, and sound editor Verna Fields for the film's crucial freeway scene. As Thompson opens fire on his unsuspecting victims, we hear only ambient noise: wind, traffic, gunshots. The effect is realistic, disturbing, and eerily prescient.

Ever the movie lover, Bogdanovich toploads *Targets* with subtle homages to golden age cinema, connecting the demise of old-school filmmaking with America's gradual loss of innocence. Byron Orlok is named after the vampire count in F. W. Murnau's horror classic *Nosferatu* (1922). Karloff is seen perusing and praising his own performance in Howard Hawks's *The Criminal Code* (1931). Thompson's doomed family watches a television ad for a showing of Otto Preminger's *Anatomy of a Murder* (1959). In a nod to the finale of *White Heat* (1949), Thompson conducts his highway massacre while perched atop an oil tank. The entrance to the now-demolished Reseda Drive-In was shot at night, aglow in 1950s neon. Children cavort on its playground while families munch popcorn and await the start of the show. A projectionist opens film cans and loads 35mm reels onto the drive-in's massive projector. Juxtaposed with the carnage on-screen, these images symbolize the end of an era.

In the TCM podcast "The Plot Thickens," Bogdanovich told Ben Mankiewicz that *Targets* evolved from an idea hatched by Roger Corman. After completing *The Terror*, Karloff still owed Corman two

A beaming Karloff pauses as ace DP László Kovács adjusts the lighting between scenes.

more days of work. At the time, Bogdanovich was employed as Corman's assistant, directing second unit material and rewriting the script for the director's biker opus *The Wild Angels* (1966). Corman offered the fledgling filmmaker $6,000 to write and direct an 80-minute feature, incorporating twenty minutes of fresh Karloff footage, twenty minutes of unused Karloff footage from *The Terror*, and forty minutes of footage with a newly chosen supporting cast.

Bogdanovich and Platt's original treatment envisioned Karloff as a masked serial killer. Harold Hayes, who'd been editing Bogdanovich's essays on film for *Esquire*, wisely advised him to scrap the script and base his story on Charles Whitman's shocking mass shooting at the University of Texas. Whitman was a boyish, twenty-five-year-old former UT Austin student and Marine Corps sharpshooter. Years of childhood abuse by his father took a terrible psychological toll. On August 1, 1966, after murdering his wife and mother, Whitman armed himself with a cache of guns and ascended the campus observation tower, killing three university employees along the way. When he reached the top, he began randomly shooting at people on the ground. Within a span of 96 minutes, he killed fourteen people and injured thirty-one more before two Austin police officers

were able to confront him and shoot him dead. The atrocity stunned Americans and prompted demands for gun control and police departments on college campuses.

Bogdanovich took Hayes's advice and rewrote his screenplay, using Whitman as a model for Bobby Thompson. Like Whitman, Thompson prepares a suicide note before beginning his rampage, methodically places his family's corpses in a bedroom, and talks about "killing some pigs." Karloff would no longer serve as the film's killer; instead, he'd portray a world-weary frightmeister ready to retire. "I laughed and I thought 'wait a second,'" Bogdanovich recalled. "If he's an actor, he doesn't want to make those kinds of movies anymore. There's the beginning of a picture." Bogdanovich also consulted his friend and idol, maverick filmmaker Samuel Fuller, who helped him shape the screenplay and suggested that the film conclude at the Reseda Drive-In with a standoff between Orlok and Thompson. (Fuller generously waived both a fee and screen credit, but Bogdanovich paid him tribute by naming Sammy Michaels after Fuller's first and middle names.) Corman served as executive producer and gave Bogdanovich a $130,000 budget and a twenty-three-day shooting schedule.

Targets was filmed without permits, forcing Bogdanovich and Kovács to "steal"

Terror Times Two: Real-life monster Thompson is juxtaposed with cinematic frightmeister Byron Orlok (Karloff).

shots throughout Los Angeles and Hollywood. The San Diego Freeway shoot ended in chaos, lending the movie some unexpected authenticity. "You're not allowed to shoot on the freeway," Bogdanovich told Mankiewicz. "We just did it." Kovács used a wide-angle lens and communicated with the director via walkie-talkies. Just before each gunshot was fired, Bogdanovich would yell "bang" into his device. "We actually brought a girl onto the freeway," he recalled. "She got out of the car in the story. And we went 'bang' and she fell, got shot in the back and fell. And that's when the cops came." As the scene ends, viewers can see the unrehearsed appearance of the police on screen. "[It] was a lot of fun," Bogdanovich remembered, "if you think of blind terror as being fun. Of all my pictures, it was the most consuming."

American International Pictures offered to release *Targets*, but Bogdanovich wanted distribution from a major studio. He showed the film to Paramount chief Robert Evans, who immediately purchased it with the approval of Gulf + Western CEO Charles Bluhdorn. Audience reception was disappointing, but stellar reviews earned the young director's debut effort a cult following. Praising *Targets* as a thriller with a social conscience, Quentin Tarantino has called it "one of the greatest directorial debuts of all time." Criterion has now released the film on Blu-ray, pristinely restored and supplemented with an analysis from Richard Linklater and informative commentaries from Bogdanovich and Platt (though Bogdanovich erroneously states that Charles Whitman committed suicide before the police could get to him).

Targets remains an essential entry in the true crime noir canon, arguably the first film based on an actual mass shooting. As a prediction of chaos to come, it remains more resonant and relevant than ever. Its many allusions to movies and filmmaking anticipate the meta-rich themes of *Day for Night* (1973), *Being John Malkovich* (1999), and *Once Upon a Time in Hollywood* (2019). Its unsparing depictions of gun violence presage *Dirty Harry* (1971) and *Taxi Driver* (1976). As film noir, its icy, documentarian approach to murder and madness recalls such films as *He Walked by Night* (1948), *Follow Me Quietly* (1949), and *Psycho* (1960). Finally, *Targets* is an exercise in irony, celebrating Hollywood's glorious past while prophesying a grim and terrifying future. ∎

BOOK vs. FILM

Mary Mallory

Married couple Mildred and Gordon Gordon turned a love for murder mysteries and the FBI into a successful novel and screenwriting career. Adapting their own crime novel *Case File: FBI* (1953) into the film noir *Down Three Dark Streets* (1954), the couple captured the repressive, anxiety-filled world of the 1950s.

Meeting at the University of Arizona, the Gordons worked as journalists before turning to novel writing. Mildred served as the editor of *Progressive Arizona*, while Gordon acted as managing editor of the *Tucson Daily Citizen*, roving correspondent for the International News Service, and publicist for 20th Century Fox. During World War II, Gordon served as a counterespionage agent for the predecessor of the Federal Bureau of Investigation, shuttling between Chicago and Washington, DC. His admiration for the FBI would permeate virtually all the couple's works. In 1947, Mildred penned a debut novel, *The Little Man*

Who Wasn't There, before the two joined forces in 1949 for the thriller *Make Haste to Live*. They would subsequently complete a new suspense novel every few years.

Doubleday published *Case File: FBI* on July 16, 1953, as a 25¢ pocket edition, with *American Magazine* condensing it for publication. Crime Club touted it as one of the year's top mysteries. Gordon explained how his personal experiences informed the novel's technical details: "In *Case File: FBI*, we attempt to draw an accurate picture of a fabulous organization at work. We took four typical but exciting cases—murder, bank robbery, auto theft and extortion— and followed them step-by-step from the day they originated on the complaint desk of the FBI's Chicago office to the capture of the guilty."

Case File: FBI focused on the crime-solving skills of scrupulous FBI special agent John "Rip" Ripley, assigned to track down the cold-blooded killer of fellow agent Zack Stewart from among the three

explosive cases Stewart was investigating at the time of his murder. The book extolled the in-depth procedures and professionalism of the bureau, whose agents modeled the motto, "Fidelity, Bravery, Integrity," with the result that the FBI raised no objections to the published work.

The ambitious production team of Jules V. Levy, Arthur Gardner, and director Arnold Laven recognized strong potential in the Gordons' suspense thriller, similar in theme and style to their previous films, *Without Warning* (1952) and *Vice Squad* (1953). Meeting in the Army Air Force's First Motion Picture Unit during World War II, the trio had formed a production company in 1951. Admiring their first two films, independent producer Edward Small financed their next, which would become *Down Three Dark Streets*, for release through United Artists. The filmmakers decided among themselves to split fees and profits, which they cross collateralized to cover losses if a later release lost money.

FBI Agent John Ripley (Broderick Crawford), Kate Martell (Ruth Roman), and her friend Dave Millson (Max Showalter/Casey Adams) meet for the first time in *Down Three Dark Streets*, as Ripley investigates who is blackmailing Martell.

Gardner purchased the rights to *Case File: FBI* for $5,000 on behalf of Challenge Pictures, Inc. during a meeting with the head of MCA's literary department, after he agreed to hire the couple to write the screenplay—their first. The duo knocked out a draft in three weeks, before producers employed veteran Bernard C. Schoenfeld, screenwriter of such film noir classics as *Phantom Lady* (1944) and *Macao* (1952), to polish the final product.

In November 1953, United Artists urged producer Small to expedite production in order to take advantage of a kidnapping wave sweeping the country: "The novel hit bookstands six months ago and is considered a particularly appropriate story. It deals with the hysterical reactions of a woman who suddenly comes into insurance money and is torn thereafter by threats against her child."

After considering stars Dana Andrews and Glenn Ford to headline the film, Levy and Gardner eventually signed burly Academy Award–winning actor Broderick Craw-

ford to play Ripley. The team quickly settled on Ruth Roman as Kate Martell, the extortion victim, for her sexy but demure allure.

Filmmakers forwarded FBI chief J. Edgar Hoover a copy of the script, to which he immediately objected, writing that he "vigorously opposed the proposed production" in a December 10, 1953, letter to the Motion Picture Production Code. On December 16, Gardner expressed surprise to the bureau's Louis Nichols, as the story presented the FBI "in a realistic and complimentary manner." The producer listed other film productions that employed more secretive bureau techniques than *Case File: FBI*, but acknowledged the creative team was willing to cooperate.

Hoover reiterated his deep reservations just before Christmas, stating that "the entire script is a blueprint for the crime of extortion." The bureau chief objected to the use of the FBI motto, the script's wiretapping scenes, and the title, stating the FBI would not provide any cooperation or

stock footage. Gardner informed the Production Code that rewrites would resolve all FBI objections.

Executive producer Small worked lean and mean, granting Levy-Gardner-Laven the same $250,000 budget as *Vice Squad*. Copying their penny-pinching success, the team relied on narration and filming on locations around the Los Angeles area like Ohrbach's department store, the new Pershing Square underground parking garage, and downtown's Sixth and Hill subway station as cost-saving measures. Gardner also negotiated a deal with Ohrbach's, employing it as Roman's office in exchange for buying wardrobe for the film at a reduced price. Beginning production in late March 1954, the feature rushed through filming in a few weeks.

Released September 1, 1954, under the more provocative title *Down Three Dark Streets*, the movie hewed closely to the original novel, employing the same character names, plot contrivances, and general outline, while streamlining the action and story into a more Dragnet-esque "just the facts" manner. Changing the location from Chicago to Los Angeles and filming semidocumentary style under the striking efforts of cinematographer Joseph Biroc strengthened the movie's visceral impact and suspense. Director Laven devised the film's look, modeled after the filmmaking technique of fellow helmsman Don Siegel.

Down Three Dark Streets employed the same three cases and characters as the novel, while altering some details for the screen. Producers toned down the book's larger-than-life Ripley into a gruff by-the-book detective, while making Roman's Martell sexier and more assertive than the thriller's devoted Korean War widow. While the book's lecherous villain, Dave Millson, devises his extortion scheme after Martell refuses his tawdry advances, Max Showalter's slick, unctuous on-screen character initiates his plot simply for greed. Where the book's Ripley records the voices of possible suspects at a dinner party of Martell's to sort out the extortionist, the filmic agent instead lifts fingerprints off guests' glasses at a birthday party to track down the culprit. The laborious, detailed procedures of the novel's FBI agents are narrowed and more refined on-screen.

Most importantly, the producers fashioned a stronger, more telling ending for the film than the book's conclusion, in which the ransom-filled suitcase is thrown off a moving train before the criminal's attempts at speeding away lead him to crash into the detective's parked car. *Down Three Dark Streets* concludes with a thrilling sequence around the actual crumbling Hollywood sign on Mount Lee in the Santa Monica Mountains. This first appearance of the gigantic billboard as a prominent set piece in a Hollywood production stands as a metaphor for the shallow, superficial dreams of the film's deluded villain. Glamorously camouflaged from a distance, up close the decrepit bulwark reveals its crude construction from leftover telephone poles, pipes, tin, and wire—a cruel, deceiving shell.

After the film's release, most of its creative personnel turned to the booming field of television to further their careers. Roman focused on the medium for the extra time and freedom it offered her as the mother of a young son. Crawford continued his fight against lawlessness by starring as Chief Dan Mathews in the massively popular TV show *Highway Patrol* (1955–59), which also extolled the bravery and expert crime-solving skills of law enforcement. Levy-Gardner-Laven would later produce such successful TV series as *The Rifleman* (1958–63), *The Detectives* (1959–62), and *The Big Valley* (1965–69), all concerned with the fight of good versus evil.

The Gordons balanced their time writing suspense novels and big and small screen adaptations of their work. They authored three more books featuring intrepid FBI agent Ripley, including one that became *Experiment in Terror* (1962), directed by Blake Edwards and scripted by the couple. The duo would gain perhaps their greatest fame with the Walt Disney film *That Darn Cat!* (1965), adapted from their 1963 book *Undercover Cat*. Known as Damn Cat or DC in the novel, the film's family friendly Siamese cat tracks the crooks and leads the FBI to save the day.

Ironically, the major set piece in *Down Three Dark Streets*—the decaying Hollywood sign—would soon eclipse both the movie and creative personnel in its celebrity. Over the next two decades, the deteriorating billboard appeared in TV shows and films such as *The Day of the Locust* (1975) and Joe Dante's B parody *Hollywood Boulevard* (1976), offering a jaded view of the Hollywood entertainment industry. In 1978, *Playboy* publisher Hugh Hefner organized a successful campaign to restore and rebuild the city landmark, which would go on to grace scores of entertainment projects and be reborn as a global icon as renowned as the Eiffel Tower or the Statue of Liberty. ∎

Martell and Ripley confront the blackmailing villain in front of the actual crumbling Hollywood Sign atop Los Angeles's Mt. Lee in the thrilling finale.

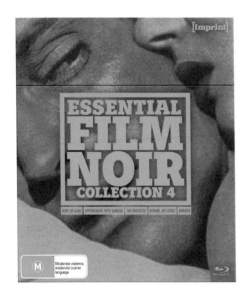

Essential Film Noir: Collection 4
(Rope of Sand / Appointment with Danger / The Enforcer / Beware, My Lovely / Jennifer) (Imprint)

Australian boutique label Imprint has been producing outstanding Blu-ray releases for years, providing beautifully mastered editions of classic and contemporary cinema with solid supplements. This set features the Blu-ray debut of two films starring Ida Lupino, with a double feature on one disc. **Beware, My Lovely** (1952) stars Robert Ryan as a soft-spoken handyman whose fragile emotional equilibrium spirals into paranoia and panic while helping war widow Lupino clean her empty rooming house over the Christmas holiday. It's their second pairing, and while they never rekindle the powerful chemistry of *On Dangerous Ground* (1951) they ably engage one another, with Lupino trying to keep her panic under control to calm the increasingly suspicious Ryan, whose quiet menace is all the more terrifying. For all the danger, it's an unexpectedly compassionate portrait of a mentally ill man. **Jennifer** (1953) is more Gothic melodrama with an edge of noir, a quietly captivating tale featuring Lupino as the new caretaker of a creaky old manor home. Elements of ghost story and murder mystery weave through the tale as the vulnerable Lupino becomes obsessed with the disappearance of the previous caretaker, her cousin Jennifer. Howard Duff (Lupino's then-husband) costars and cinematographer James Wong Howe helps director Joel Newton create an eerie, haunted atmosphere. Both films are mastered from new 4K scans, though you will see signs of frame damage and tears on *Beware, My Lovely.*

The other three are upgrades from earlier US Blu-ray releases, mastered from new 4K scans from Paramount. Set in the unforgiving desert badlands and cutthroat diamond trade of North Africa, **Rope of Sand** (1949) stars Burt Lancaster as a bitter American out for vengeance while costars Claude Rains, Paul Henreid, and Peter Lorre could be the mercenary evil twins of their *Casablanca* characters. Director William Dieterle nicely shifts from the hard daylight of the desert to the nocturnal world. **Appointment with Danger** (1950) stars Alan Ladd as a hard-boiled postal inspector knocked off-balance by a witness to murder: a sunny, sweet nun (Phyllis Calvert) with a taste for adventure. The generic thriller is more *policier* than film noir but features plenty of cynical patter and Jack Webb and Harry Morgan as a murderous criminal duo. Humphrey Bogart is a crusading district attorney in **The Enforcer** (1951), a noir-influenced update of the Warner Bros. gangster classics inspired by the real-life case against Murder, Inc. Director Bretaigne Windust gives the film a semidocumentary look with shadowy urban scenes and an atmosphere of social corruption, and an uncredited Raoul Walsh delivers the dynamic opening and closing sequences.

SUPPLEMENTS: *Beware, My Lovely* features commentary by Jason Ney and a featurette on Lupino featuring film historian Pamela Hutchinson. *Rope of Sand* offers commentary by Samm Deighan and *Appointment with Danger* and *The Enforcer* feature commentary by Frank Krutnik. All show increased detail and clarity from earlier Olive Blu-rays.

All of these discs will also be made available individually in September 2023.

—*Sean Axmaker*

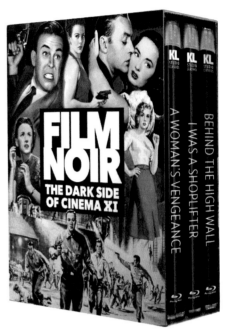

Film Noir: The Dark Side of Cinema XI
(A Woman's Vengeance / I Was a Shoplifter / Behind the High Wall) (Kino)

Film Noir: The Dark Side of Cinema XII
(Undertow / Outside the Wall / Hold Back Tomorrow) (Kino)

Film Noir: The Dark Side of Cinema XIII
(Spy Hunt / The Night Runner / Step Down to Terror) (Kino)

Film Noir: The Dark Side of Cinema XIV
(Undercover Girl / One Way Street / Appointment with a Shadow) (Kino)

Four new box sets from Kino Lorber collect a dozen programmers from Universal, featuring mostly second-tier stars like Scott Brady, Charles Drake, and George Nader. Their claims to noir vary by film but most have something of interest for film

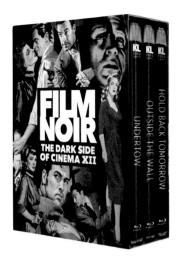
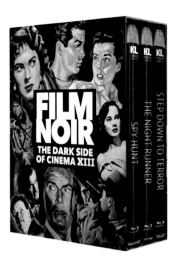
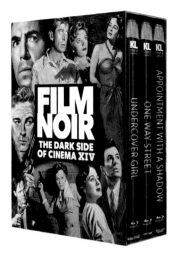

noir fans and all of them look terrific (nine feature new masters).

Charles Boyer is the patient, long-suffering husband of a bitter invalid in **A Woman's Vengeance** (1948), a mix of murder mystery and Gothic melodrama that channels *Gaslight* (1944). Scripted by Aldous Huxley and directed by Zoltan Korda, it's awkwardly plotted and suffers a passive, melancholy performance by Boyer as the dutiful husband at the mercy of vengeful women. Jessica Tandy provides the film's only real passion, which the film dramatizes in a magnificent storm that accompanies her outpouring of emotion. If only the rest of the film carried that charge. **I Was a Shoplifter** (1950) goes for a docudrama quality in its tale of an undercover investigator (Scott Brady) on the trail of a massive shoplifting ring, but journeyman director Charles Lamont doesn't have much to work with. Look for Tony Curtis as pretty-boy henchman Pepe and Rock Hudson in a bit part. There's more potential in **Behind the High Wall** (1956), with eternal supporting player Tom Tully in the lead as a frustrated prison warden whose impulsive theft of stolen loot leaves an innocent victim (John Gavin) holding the bag. Character actor turned filmmaker Abner Biberman never fully commits to the potential as Tully's idealist turns cynical and the unjustly convicted bystander is chewed up in the predatory prison culture.

William Castle directs **Undertow** (1949), a snappy little thriller starring Scott Brady as an ex-con and former gambler ready to start a new life away from the rackets. Then he's framed for murder, sending him scrambling to prove his innocence. Castle shifts from redemption drama to nightmare noir, punching up the simple story with abrupt explosions of violence and enough momentum to keep you caught up in Brady's flight. Richard Basehart is the ex-con trying to go straight in **Outside the Wall** (1950), a solid mix of social drama and noir thriller that gets the determined parolee tangled up in the scramble for a fortune in stolen cash. Basehart is terrific as a guy who spent half his life in stir and falls back on those prison instincts, and writer-director Crane Wilbur makes his journey as central as the seduction and double crosses of the plot. **Hold Back Tomorrow** (1955) is an odd entry in the US filmography of Czech-born filmmaker-actor Hugo Haas, a two-hander starring a bitter, combustible John Agar as a death row inmate and longtime Haas leading lady Cleo Moore as the suicidal escort hired to fulfill the condemned man's last wish. It's like a noir fairy tale, complete with an offbeat romance, by way of a B-movie morality play. I can't say Agar and Moore are good but they add to the bizarre fantasy's offbeat dynamic.

Spy Hunt (1950) is a Cold War thriller featuring Howard Duff as an American in Europe, a hidden cache of microfilm, an international cast of spies, and two escaped black panthers in the Swiss Alps (doubled by California). While the plot is routine, director George Sherman provides some nicely staged moments, including the feral beauty of the cats in motion, and lets Duff's easy charm and American practicality anchor the spy thriller. **The Night Runner** (1957) is a straight social drama with a twist of domestic thriller. Ray Danton is a man released from an overcrowded mental hospital who cracks under the pressure of everyday life in a sleepy California coastal town. Best intentions are lost in the routine script and indifferent direction by Abner Biberman. Costar Colleen Miller takes top billing in **Step Down to Terror** (1958), a low-budget take on the original story that Hitchcock and Thornton Wilder transformed into *Shadow of a Doubt* (1943). Charles Drake, however, is no Joseph Cotten and the bland direction and script exposition make his psychosis less interesting.

James Mason and Dan Duryea help Argentine filmmaker Hugo Fregonese (making his first US feature) elevate **One Way Street** (1950), which takes Mason's corrupt doctor to a remote Mexican village where he rediscovers his lost hope. It's framed, however, with a film noir simmering with greed, betrayal, and vengeance. Fregonese masterfully creates tension from Mason's underplayed surgeon, Duryea's arrogant gang leader, and William Conrad's seemingly easygoing henchman who endures Duryea's insolence. **Undercover Girl** (1950) stars Alexis Smith as a rookie cop who infiltrates a drug ring and Scott Brady as the head of the task force. Director Joseph Pevney punctuates the otherwise serviceable cop drama with jolts of brutal violence and a shadowy climax, and Royal Dano is memorable as a shifty underworld character named the Moocher. **Appointment with a Shadow** (1957) is a twist on a classic setup: the unreliable witness hunted by a killer that nobody believes is real. George Nader goes full *Lost Weekend* as the alcoholic reporter whose scoop takes an abrupt turn when he becomes the inconvenient witness to a frame-up. The minor pleasures include Brian Keith as an affable cop whose indulgence of an unreliable drunk defies common sense.

EXTRAS: Commentary on nine discs, including FNF board member Alan K. Rode on *Outside the Wall*; Jason Ney on *A Woman's Vengeance*; Ney with Scott Brady's son, Tim Tierney, on *Undertow*; a chatty David DeCoteau with historian David Del Valle on *Appointment with a Shadow*; as well as *Spy Hunt*, *The Night Runner*, *Step Down to Terror*, *One Way Street*, and *Undercover Girl*.

—*Sean Axmaker*

BOOK REVIEWS

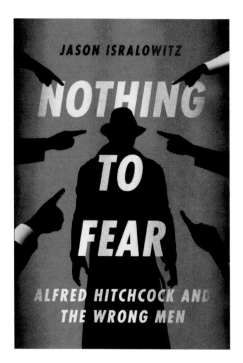

Nothing to Fear: Alfred Hitchcock and the Wrong Men

By Jason Isralowitz
Fayetteville Mafia Press, January 2023
250 pages

The Wrong Man, the most true-to-life picture that Alfred Hitchcock ever filmed, begins with a lie. At the end of the opening credits, tiny print at the bottom of the screen declares that "the story, all names, characters, and incidents portrayed in this production are fictitious."

In fact, just about every character in the 1956 film is based on a real person. Many scenes were filmed at the locations where they happened, from jail to courtroom to nightclub. Presumably, someone at the studio failed to update the disclaimer. This inadvertent error didn't have any lasting negative effects: no harm, no foul. But sometimes, innocent mistakes can have enormous consequences. This is especially true in film noir. Fate—the genre's eternal obsession—doesn't like to let us off easy.

Consider the nightmarish story of Manny Balestrero, a Queens musician whose ordinary life was halted in January 1953 when people trying to do the right thing accused him of sticking up an insur-

ance office the previous year. He gets put through the wringer in The Wrong Man, which is remarkably accurate as far as Hollywood productions go. Manhattan lawyer Jason Isralowitz emphasizes this accuracy in his revealing and insightful new book Nothing to Fear: Alfred Hitchcock and the Wrong Men.

Balestrero was nearly convicted based on testimony from mistaken eyewitnesses and an extraordinary bit of bad luck regarding a stick-up note. He was hardly an outlier, as Isralowitz writes. In the mid-twentieth century, many innocent people fell victim to "witness coaching, prejudicial identification procedures, and the withholding of exculpatory information." Nothing to Fear exposes the rampant mishandling of criminal cases in the New York region and reveals a system that repeatedly refused to reform itself or take responsibility for its mistakes. Unsurprisingly, newspapers were much more interested in white victims of mistaken prosecution like Balestrero, who was so unassuming that he was portrayed by the cinema's patron saint of everymens: Henry Fonda. As Isralowitz notes, Hollywood and the media didn't care about the plight of those who faced bigotry and didn't have access to sharp attorneys.

The exhaustive detail regarding these cases can at times bog down the narrative of the book, and movie buffs may choose to quickly skim these passages until Isralowitz focuses engagingly on the making of Hitchcock's film. The movie is an oddity for a number of reasons, and lacks several of Hitch's trademarks: there's no sexual tension, barely any suspense, and only a brief glimmer of humor. Overall, the movie "proves once again that life can be more interminable than fiction," jibed the Los Angeles Times, although fans have praised how Hitchcock deeply explored his obsessions with false accusations and the transference of guilt. And its real-life plot gave the director a chance to scare us in a new way: this, he makes it clear, could happen to anyone, not just beautiful people in beautiful places.

Isralowitz finds nifty details about the making of the movie. Hitchcock was wed-

ded to his storyboards; an actor playing a detective needed elevator shoes to appear as tall as Fonda; and preproduction research with the Balestrero family and others was intensive. Readers will also learn about a movie-related bombing plot and the bizarre appearance by Balestrero on the game show To Tell the Truth (1956–68) in 1957. As for the film's larger themes, the author believes The Wrong Man is "one of the most important movies about criminal justice ever made." It's more accurate to say it's one of the most *revealing* movies about criminal justice.

In real life, the effects of the accusations against Balestrero were even more devastating than shown on screen. Balestrero's son, Greg, now an executive, tells the author that "it was like tossing a hand grenade in an Easter dinner . . . everybody had to choose: guilty or not guilty. There were people who started to take sides, and that affected us in a big way."

The movie also whitewashes the story of Balestrero's wife, Rose, played by Vera Miles. Isralowitz finds that she most definitely did *not* recover from a mental breakdown, despite a postscript at the end of the film stating otherwise. Even so, Hitchcock's fidelity to reality does tell us important things about the plight of the innocent who are targeted by the justice system.

The detective in The Wrong Man is lying when he says the innocent have "nothing to fear." Anyone can get swept up by bogus accusations and bad luck, let alone unfair investigative techniques and purposeful misconduct. Hitchcock understood that oftentimes, the scariest monsters under the bed are the ones wearing badges.

—Randy Dotinga

NOIR CROSSWORD

Noir Vrai

Rich Taus

ACROSS

1. Long, involved stories
6. Kind of committee
11. Successors to LPs
14. What Adrian Messenger left in a John Huston mystery
15. "I praise" in Imperial Rome
16. Small battery
17. She has the title role in 29. Across
19. Rugby analog of a touchdown
20. Head honcho, briefly
21. Desert respites
23. Radius of a wheel
26. Yoga position
29. Neo-noir inspired by 43. Across (2006)
34. *The ___ Bunch,* a blended family
35. Like Vassar but not Bryn Mawr
36. 1946 film about the CIA precursor
37. Supremes leader
38. Littlest littermates
39. *___ Fiction* (1994)
40. *Cakes and ___*
41. To be used as ear drops
42. Inlets
43. Victim of a lurid 1947 murder
47. Serrated, like a leaf edge
48. Dead men don't tell them
49. Mel with a thousand voices
52. Light prefix in a noirish 1944 film
53. Set in *Rocky Horror Picture Show*
54. 29. Across actress with two Oscars
62. HI strings
63. Susan Lucci's daytime femme fatale
64. Source of Kollywood (Tamil) neo-noir
65. Anago or unagi
66. Gave an R
67. Lina Wertmuller's ___ *Away* (1974)

DOWN

1. Spade

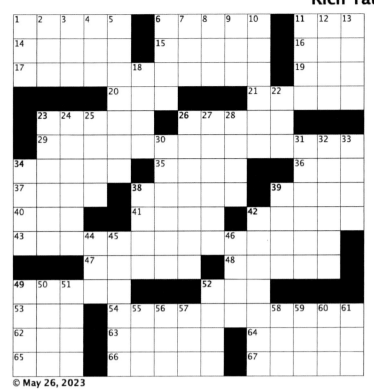

© May 26, 2023

2. 2001 Will Smith biopic
3. Scala of *The Garment Jungle*
4. Set a price of
5. Remain loyal to
6. Part of aka
7. Well, lah-di- ___
8. Enemy in *Mulan*
9. ___ *to Billie Joe*
10. Cerveza often served with lime
11. Widely reviled film of 2019
12. Alternative to truth
13. *Murder, He ___,* 1945 black comedy
18. Old unit for a film's runtime
22. Sound to show the uvula
23. Amble
24. Early part of a drug trial
25. Weighty Brit. ref. books
26. Poisonous plant, anagram of "a notice"
27. SNL segment
28. Does basic math
30. Accents that belong in "cinema verite"
31. Site of a murder in *The Da Vinci Code*

32. Keys
33. Venomous Nile snakes
34. Hillside overlooking a loch
38. Cop or call prefix
39. *The Drowning ___* (1975)
42. Auto frame
44. "...and now, your moment of ___"
45. Animated espionage sitcom
46. Legal postponement
49. Color in a 1946 noir title similar to 29. Across
50. 49. Down film's Veronica or Johansson's role in 29. Across
51. Victim of fratricide
52. Alum
55. Org. in 1947 noir *Odd Man Out*
56. Comp. ___
57. Noirish ___ *in the Hole* (1951)
58. 45 degrees from a Hitchcock heading
59. Citrus drink suffix
60. Minibar liquor bottle
61. Actress Dennings

For solution, go to filmnoirfoundation.org

Made in the USA
Middletown, DE
12 October 2023

40697772R00042